W9-CEW-128

Holy Cow!

The Life and Times of Halsey Hall

Holy Cow!

The Life and Times of Halsey Hall

BY STEW THORNLEY

Foreword by Sue Hall Kennedy

NODIN PRESS
Minneapolis

Library of Congress Catalog Card No. 90-92230
ISBN 0-931714-43-5

Nodin Press, a division of Micawber's, Inc.
525 North Third Street
Minneapolis, MN 55401

Printed in U.S.A. at
Gopher State Litho, Minneapolis, MN

Also by Stew Thornley

On to Nicollet:
The Glory and Fame of the Minneapolis Millers

Basketball's Original Dynasty:
The History of the Lakers

Acknowledgments

"Anything for Halsey" was a refrain I heard often as I spoke with people who had known and dealt with Halsey Hall.

Some were busy, others had pressing problems to deal with, but all were able to find at least a few minutes to rattle off stories and firsthand memories of Halsey. And before they finished, they would often give me the names of other people to contact. The list of people to interview grew quickly and, as word spread about what I was doing, people began calling me.

Without the assistance of the people and organizations listed below, this biography would not have been possible. These are the folks who were willing to do "Anything for Halsey."

Many thanks to:

George Rekela, Brenda Himrich, and Dave Gade for their tremendous support, encouragement, and advice throughout this entire project.

Ken Ottoson, Larry Loeschen, and Frank Engdahl for the use of their tape-recorded interviews with Halsey.

Members of the Halsey Hall Chapter of the Society for American Baseball Research: Jim Wyman, Alan Holst, Paul Rittenhouse, Stan Carlson, Don Wiese, Fred Souba, Bob Evans, Glenn Gostick, Dave Anderson, Don Rittenhouse, John DiMeglio, Rosemary Palmer, Marshall Tanick, Nancy Jo Leachman, Joe O'Connell, Alden Mead, and Howard Luloff.

Family members and personal friends of the Hall and Kennedy families: Norene Becker, Barbara Ely, Naomi Ward, Kathryn Heine, Dorothy MacIver Pearson, Myrt Harrison, and Ruth Hirshfield Heidelberg.

Halsey's former colleagues in newspaper and radio

work: Ray Scott, Stew MacPherson, Jimmy Byrne, Don Riley, Patrick Reusse, Bob Beebe, Tom Mee, Roger Erickson, Dave Shama, Ray Christensen, Frank Buetel, Bob DeHaven, Jack Horner, Bob Lundegaard, Dave Mona, Dick Gordon, Dick Jonckowski, Irv Letofsky, Bob Wolff, Joe Hennessey, Joe Soucheray, Larry Jagoe, Dick Enroth, Rollie Johnson, E. W. Ziebarth, Joyce Lamont, Herb Carneal, Jon Roe, Tom Jardine, Mark Tierney and Larry Haeg, Jr.

Community leaders who were associated with Halsey: Norm McGrew, Don Stolz, Harvey O'Phelen, Bob Sorenson, Art Solz, Dr. Andrew W. Shea, Dennis Blenis, Harvey Mackay, and Harry Davis.

Upper Midwest athletes and sports figures: Bill Daley, Pug Lund, Babe LeVoir, Ed Widseth, Stan Kostka, Pete Deanovic, Paul Giel, George Mikan, Angelo Giuliani, Marsh Ryman, Jules Perlt, Calvin Griffith, Ray Crump, Irv Nerdahl, George Brophy, Murray Warmath, Wayne (Red) Williams, Earl Battey, Gene Mauch, and Al Worthington.

Wayne Courtney and John Sammon, who officiated sporting events with Halsey for many years.

Bob Cronk, David Pollock, Patricia Palmer, and Mark Stengel, fans who shared their memories of Halsey.

Steve Enck and Paul Bergly of WCCO Radio and Dave Moore of WCCO Television.

John Duxbury of *The Sporting News.*

John Kuenster, editor of *Baseball Digest.*

Larry Ritter, author of *The Glory of Their Times.*

John Baule of the Hennepin County Historical Society, Deonna M. Ard of the Kansas City Public Library, Cary M. Mazer of the American Society for Theatre Research, Elizabeth Bailey of the State Historical Society of Missouri, Ted Hathaway of the Minneapolis

Public Library, Dorothy Swerdlove of the Billy Rose Theatre Collection, James F. Caccamo of the Hudson (Ohio) Library and Historical Society, Evelyn M. Peck of the Portage County (Ohio) Historical Society, Bill Brophy of the *Wisconsin State Journal,* and the staffs of the Minneapolis History Collection and the Minnesota Historical Society.

And most of all, Halsey's daughter, Sue Hall Kennedy, who inherited both her dad's fabulous memory and his gift for telling stories.

Foreword

By Sue Hall Kennedy

This is definitely not a "Daddy Dearest" foreword, but rather the exact opposite. Growing up with Daddy meant laughter, love, cigars, *and* onions, of course. It was like living in a glass house, and I loved it!

I enjoyed being the daughter of a local celebrity. It was sheer delight to walk down the street with him and have people say "Hi" or wave as we passed by. I'd be so proud seeing all these people come up and ask for his autograph when he was the master of ceremonies (best in the Midwest) or the main speaker at a sports banquet.

Daddy's gone now, but I still have the wonderful memories. Some of the most enjoyable involved going to spring training with the Minneapolis Millers' baseball team from the time I was ten years old until I was 21. It was exciting to have the various players help me with my homework!

Dad loved parties, and he and my mom (a gourmet cook) gave the best. The parties usually contained a rousing game of bridge. I'd fill in for him when he drove downtown for his five-minute radio show, "Time Out for Sports with Halsey Hall," at 10:25 P.M. He always made it back to the bridge game in record time. This was one of the few occasions he wouldn't stop to pick green onions out of the garden before coming into the house.

Dad and I were quite a comedy team. During these parties, we often performed blackouts (short skits) together.

Dad loved surprises. One of my favorite's came when he invited Andy Cohen—a former second baseman for the Millers who was then the manager of the Denver Bears baseball team—to one of our parties. It was a wonderful treat to again see Andy, who used to help me with my algebra when I was in ninth grade.

Then there was the time when, the night before my husband and I were going on a Twins' road trip to Washington, D.C. with Dad, he told us that we'd be meeting the president, Lyndon Johnson. It was delightful meeting him and telling him our name was Kennedy.

My friends became Dad's friends. He would often substitute at my Morningside Woman's Club bridge group. There he was playing bridge with 15 women (and yes, they let him smoke his cigar). He had the most infectious laugh. He'd come to plays I was performing in and sit in the middle of the audience. When he started to laugh, the rest of the audience laughed, too. It did wonders for our comedies!

When I was a student at the University of Minnesota, he was always the guest speaker at my Alpha Omicron Pi Sorority's annual Dad's Day luncheon, which preceded one of the Gopher football games. (Naturally, he waived his usual speaker's fee.) He was even the surprise guest speaker at our son's high-school graduation breakfast, appearing at three o'clock in the morning. What a sport!

Dad deeply loved his family, and he expressed those feeling in poems he wrote to Mother and me. Here's a short example of his poetic side:

> *I was dreaming, oh my sweethearts*
> *Of a kingdom far away;*
> *Where love and laughter flourish*
> *And hearts are always gay.*

I wandered there, my darlings,
So happy and carefree,
Because, you see, my loved ones,
You wandered there with me.

Perhaps it's fitting that my husband and I now live in Tampa, Florida, the cigar capital of the world, and our two daughters and a son-in-law live in Orlando, just a few miles away from the "It's a Small, Small World" ride at Walt Disney World, a favorite attraction of Dad and Mom's.

Our son, daughter-in-law, and grandson are keeping the Minnesota home fires burning in Golden Valley.

The late Dick Cullum, Dad's co-worker and friend, wanted to write a book on him, but Dad just didn't have the inclination to do the background work. Voila! Thirteen years later, along comes Stew Thornley, an enthusiastic young man, skilled writer, and avid baseball fan who has served two terms as president of the Halsey Hall Chapter of the Society for American Baseball Research. Stew has uncovered a great deal of interesting information about Dad's ancestors that I never knew, especially about his mother, an acclaimed stage actress. You'll also learn why becoming a newspaper man came naturally to Dad.

I hope this foreword has whet your appetite and that you're now ready to sit back, relax, and enjoy *Holy Cow! The Life and Times of Halsey Hall.*

Sue Hall Kennedy

Table of Contents

Preface

Halsey had always been there. For those of my generation whose first baseball memories consist of listening to Minnesota Twins' broadcasts in the 1960s, Halsey Hall was an institution. And as we listened to his raucous laughter mixed in with stories of the Minneapolis Millers and St. Paul Saints from long ago, we just assumed he'd always be there.

That wasn't to be, of course, but I consider myself fortunate that before he did leave us, I had the chance to meet him on a handful of occasions.

The first time was in July of 1963, on the eve of my eighth birthday. Passing through Milwaukee on a family vacation, we stayed at the Schroeder Hotel, which, by sheer coincidence, was housing the Minnesota Twins, who were in town to play an exhibition game against the Braves that evening.

The lobby was loaded with Twins—Earl Battey, Camilo Pascual, Bernie Allen—but the first person my brother and I sought out was Halsey, who was sitting on a couch nearby with his eyes closed. We weren't sure if he was actually sleeping or not, but as we drifted closer, he seemed to sense our presence and opened his eyes. If he was bothered by a couple of kids interrupting his rest, he showed no indication of it. Instead, he talked baseball with us for a few minutes and concluded the conversation by saying he hoped we enjoyed the game that night.

We did. Harmon Killebrew beat Hank Aaron in a pre-game home run hitting contest and the Twins beat the Braves, 5-2, but our fondest memory of that day remained our chat with Halsey.

It was the first but not the last contact I was to have

with Halsey. Over the next few years I developed an interest in the professional baseball teams that played in Minnesota before the Twins and, on several occasions, wrote to Halsey with questions about the Minneapolis Millers. He answered every letter.

Then, in 1969, when I was batboy for the Minnesota Gopher baseball team, I was invited to be a guest on Halsey's pre-game television show. One of the features of the show was a chance to stump Halsey with a baseball question. Many of the questions he received from guests bordered on the ridiculous, such as "How many runs were scored against the Philadelphia Phillies last year?" Halsey was good, but nobody's that good.

I wanted a question that would at least give him a fighting chance, so I came up with one regarding the Gophers' longtime coach, Dick Siebert. "How many Big Ten titles have the Gophers won under Dick Siebert?" I asked.

Halsey rolled the question around in his mind for a few seconds and then took an educated guess. "Seven." He was right.

I didn't receive the grand prize, a gift certificate for a luggage store, but I did receive a consolation gift of a couple of movie passes.

Baby boomers may remember Halsey only as an announcer with the Twins, but he had a colorful career in both radio and newspaper work long before the Twins moved to Minnesota.

He had many trademarks—his boisterous laugh as well as his love of green onions and cigars—and stories about him abound. Some memories have gone to the grave with those who knew him best. But, fortunately, there are many friends, relatives, and acquaintances still here whose memories and stories of Halsey are endless. And even many who have departed did not go without first leaving a few memories behind.

The sources were diverse, but plentiful enough that a biography was possible on Halsey Hall, one of the Upper Midwest's greatest characters and one of its most popular and best-loved residents.

Halsey Hall began using "Holy Cow!" on baseball broadcasts in the 1930s.

The Original Holy Cow

For some fans, the debate regarding the first announcer to use the expression "Holy Cow!" on a baseball broadcast comes down to two men: New York Yankees' shortstop-turned-broadcaster Phil Rizzuto, and Harry Caray, who has called the play-by-play for the St. Louis Cardinals, Oakland Athletics, Chicago White Sox, and Chicago Cubs.

Caray himself lays claim to the honor, citing evidence that he first uttered the expression while announcing a semi-pro baseball tournament in Battle Creek, Michigan, in the early 1940s at a time when Rizzuto was still in the Yankee infield and not yet in the broadcast booth.

But another announcer was hollering "Holy Cow!" on baseball broadcasts long before Caray entered the profession. Halsey Hall started his play-by-play announcing for the Minneapolis Millers in 1934 and was using the expression from the start.

Don Rittenhouse, a lifelong Minneapolis resident who began following the Millers in the 1930s, says he has clear memories of Halsey blurting "Holy Cow!" in response to home runs hit by the Millers' great slugger, Joe Hauser. Hauser's career in Minneapolis ran through 1936, several years before Harry Caray first sat behind a microphone.

But while Halsey might not have had the chance to utter the phrase over the airwaves until the mid-1930s, he, in fact, had adopted the expression nearly 20 years before. He picked up the term, appropriately enough, on the baseball diamond.

Halsey's first exposure to baseball came when his father, an itinerant newspaperman/publicity agent on one of his infrequent stops at home, took him to Nicollet Park on Decoration Day in 1909. Legend has it that his father, declaring that "No son of mine is going to be a sissy and not like baseball!", had to spank the boy before he agreed to attend. It was to be the last time Halsey Hall ever needed any persuasion to attend a baseball game. After watching the Millers beat the St. Paul Saints, 3-0, Halsey was hooked. It's possible that from this time on he had to be spanked to keep him *away* from the ball park.

Like many of his baseball-crazy friends, Halsey did whatever was necessary to stay close to the game. The lads became experts at finding ways of gaining free admittance to Nicollet Park. Chasing down a foul ball that flew out of the park and turning it in at the gate was one way. But before long, Halsey had found another.

He would serve as batboy for the visiting team or else just show up a few hours before a game and volunteer to help mow the outfield grass. In 1915 the Millers acquired veteran catcher Billy Sullivan, a saintly man whose strongest expletive was "Holy Cow!" A member of the Chicago White Sox "Hitless Wonders" team that won the World Series in 1906, Sullivan by this time was in the twilight of his career and trying to hang on in the professional ranks as long as he could. Sullivan spent only one year in Minneapolis, but it was long enough for a young batboy to pick up some of his idiom. Before the season was over, "Holy Cow!" had been transferred from Billy Sullivan to Halsey Hall.

"Holy Cow!" became a familiar phrase to sports fans in the Upper Midwest as its user became one of the area's most beloved citizens as well as one of its more colorful characters.

In the public eye for more than half-a-century, Halsey

juggled fulltime careers as a newspaper reporter and radio announcer; along the way, he somehow found the time to moonlight as a referee and as a public speaker.

Halsey was regarded as the dean of Twin Cities sportswriters, and his vivid and descriptive writing style helped to establish a following from coast to coast. As a radio announcer, Halsey had a sports program so popular that pilots reported seeing the lights in homes darken in droves when the show ended at 10:30 each evening.

Stories of his antics and idiosyncrasies abound, and he was much sought after for his fabulous memory, which allowed him to recount sports sagas from earlier eras.

Halsey is the man who gave the University of Minnesota football team the nickname "Golden Gophers," the man most frequently called upon to settle a sports wager, and the man who could always find the light side in even the grimmest of contests.

Halsey was also the man at the microphone when the Minnesota Twins played their first game in 1961. For 12 years, Halsey didn't miss a pitch as he was on hand for the nearly two thousand games the Twins played during that period.

"He was the most unforgettable man I've ever known," said Twins' slugger Harmon Killebrew.

"A living legend among the sports fraternity," is the description bestowed upon Halsey by Ray Scott, Halsey's partner on Twins' broadcasts from 1961-66.

Through it all, Halsey remained loyal to his favorite expression. Did it ever bother him that others, such as Caray and Rizzuto, have received the credit for originating "Holy Cow"? His daughter, Sue Kennedy, says she can't recall that it ever did, but a couple of his colleagues remember it as a sore spot with Halsey.

"It rankled him, I know, that Harry Caray was given the credit for first using it," said Ray Christensen, who broadcast both Twins' and Minnesota Gopher football games with Halsey.

On that subject, Ray Scott added, "Halsey was never one to complain a lot about anything, but that definitely bothered him."

If he was aggravated by the matter, however, for the most part he kept it to himself. That was his nature.

In some parts of the country, the term may be associated with other announcers, but in the Upper Midwest the expression remains synonomous with Halsey Hall, sports aficionado and purveyor of the original "Holy Cow!"

Halsey's Roots

The path Halsey Hall followed in his life may well have been determined at an early age. How much a part heredity played in the interests he developed and the aptitudes he displayed is debatable, but there is no doubt that a number of his proclivities were also present in his ancestors, many of whom were prominent citizens in their own rights.

Halsey's maternal grandfather, Henry P. White, was a distinguished Missouri judge. Descended from Irish and Scotch-Irish stock, White was born in Potsdam, New York on January 13, 1841. After being admitted to the bar at the age of 24, he came west, stopping in Chicago and St. Louis before settling in Kansas City. In October 1874 he was appointed Judge of the Criminal Court of Jackson County and was elected to fill that office at each judicial election thereafter until his death in 1892.

Judge White was married in 1875 to Euphemia (Effie) deLuce and had three children, including a daughter who was to become Halsey's mother as well as the probable source of his later love of theater. Mary deLuce White yearned for a career on the stage almost from the moment of her birth in 1876. She made the most of her aspirations, becoming a renowned Shakespearean actress, sharing the stage with Helena Modjeska in her 1901 debut on Broadway and later performing with E. H. Sothern, Julia Marlowe, and Walter Hampden.

Mary Hall (even though she separated from Halsey's father before reaching stardom, she retained the family name throughout her theatrical career) was in constant demand in both Boston and New York, but attracted a following in several other cities as well. She went to London with the New York-based Arizona Company, and upon her return to America, undertook stock work, becoming the leading woman of the Empire Theatre in Boston and later of the Pike Theatre Company in Cincinnati.

"Her first part was that of Glory Quayle in 'The Christian,' and this she played so superbly that then and there she won the hearts of all who heard her," wrote the *Cincinnati Commercial Gazette* of her work with the Pike Company. "She was extremely versatile, taking the part of child, girl, and older woman with the same ease and grace.

"She played the leading parts constantly and gained steadily in popularity, until she was by far the chief attraction there.

"She had not only beauty, but a winning intellect and a charming personality. Her admirers flocked to hear her, and she fairly lived in a bower of bouquets during her engagement here, so profuse were her friends in their remembrances."

By the 1920s, Mary Hall was being described by many in theater circles as "the most famous stock actress living." She was nothing if not versatile, adapting to a variety of leading men, both on the stage and in real life.

Despite being married seven times, it did not appear that her plans ever included motherhood. Even though a son was produced from her first marriage, she did not allow the boy to interfere with her ambitions. After separating from, and eventually divorcing, her first husband, she was to see little of her son, and it would be left to others to raise Halsey.

The family tree on Halsey's father's side can be traced to colonial America. Halsey's great-great-great-grandfather, Jabez Hall, was a first lieutenant in the Fourth Company for the British colony of Connecticut in the 1760s. Along with his father, Jabez fought in the American Revolution, serving as a lieutenant in the Continental Army, while the elder Hall reached the rank of captain.

It was Jabez's son who became the first of several in the clan to bear the euphonic name of Halsey Hall. The original Halsey fought in the War of 1812 and saw action in the Battle of Sackett's Harbor, New York.

Next in the family line was Lyman Walcott Hall, who was born in Lanesboro, Berkshire County, Massachusetts on March 9, 1808. In 1830 Lyman moved to Ravenna, Ohio and became the first member of the Hall family to enter the newspaper trade, a profession that would pass from father to son (or sons) through the next four generations. A staunch abolitionist, Lyman purchased an interest in, and eventually became sole proprietor of, an anti-slavery newspaper in Ravenna, the *Ohio Star*. In 1844, he campaigned unsuccessfully for Congress, running as a member of the Free Soil Party. Lyman had six children—two who died shortly after birth, as well as two daughters, Harriet W. and Laura W., and a pair of sons, Harlan P. and Halsey R. W.

Halsey R. W. (the initials stood for Roger Wing) Hall, the grandson of one Halsey and the grandfather of another, was born August 3, 1834 in Hudson, Ohio, but grew up in Ravenna, 15 miles to the southeast. He followed his father into the newspaper business and, in the process, cultivated acquaintanceships with many of the state's most prominent families, including the Garfields of nearby Hiram. Halsey and his first wife, Jane, had four children, but only two who lived beyond infancy—Ann S. and Smith B., who was to become Halsey Lewis Hall's father.

Born in Ravenna on June 29, 1858, Smith Bagg Hall attended Adelbert College of Western Reserve University in Hudson and, shortly after graduating, used some family connections to land a job in Washington, D. C. Over the objections of his father, who did not approve of his son entering government work, Smith found a position in the pension department through the efforts of James A. Garfield, who had just been elected president of the United States. Meanwhile, Halsey R. W.'s younger brother, Harlan Page Hall, was becoming the first in the family to establish roots, as well as notoriety, in Minnesota.

Harlan was still in Ohio in 1861 when he married Harriet Lamb, a woman afflicted with pulmonary consumption. Hearing that the climate of Minnesota was favorable to those who suffered from this disease, Harlan wrote to Henry A. Swift, a native of Ravenna, who was living in St. Peter, Minnesota and serving in the state senate at the time. Swift, who became Governor of Minnesota the following year, gave such a fine description of the state that Harlan and Harriet decided to move to St. Paul in October of 1862.

Harlan P. Hall worked briefly as a compositor for the *St. Paul Press*. Three years later he and a partner, John X. Davidson, purchased another newspaper, the *St. Paul Pioneer* (which later became the *St. Paul Pioneer Press*) for $25,000. Although they retained ownership of the *Pioneer* for less than a year, Harlan stayed in the newspaper game and made it his career.

Described as a "political and journalistic maverick," Harlan spent his life trying to further the cause of the Democratic party, and it was toward this end that he founded the *St. Paul Dispatch* in 1868. He sold the *Dispatch* in 1876 to a stock company, which promptly shifted the newspaper's politics to support the Republican Party.

Two years later, Harlan founded another Democratic paper, the *St. Paul Globe*, and in 1882 started two more dailies in an attempt to help Charles Kindred of Brainerd in his race for the United States Congress.

Minnesota's Fifth Congressional District, which covered the northern half of the state at the time, was strongly Scandinavian. Despite his enormous wealth, Kindred was a distinct underdog to Knute Nelson of Alexandria, a native of Norway who had the support of the region's newspapers. In an attempt to counteract this advantage, Kindred not only bought three weekly papers but also asked Harlan P. Hall to start daily newspapers in Fergus Falls and Duluth.

As it happened, Halsey R. W. was in the process of moving to Minnesota and was staying with his brother at the time. Viewing this as an opportunity to get his son out of Washington, Halsey prevailed upon Harlan to put Smith in charge of one of the newspapers.

"My uncle said it would be all right, and I could have either one I wanted," recalled Smith in a 1916 interview. "Oddly enough, my father picked out Fergus Falls as the more desirable of the two cities, and the one which was going to have the greatest future. So I came out from Washington, with no experience and no equipment except that of belonging to a third generation of newspaper men, and my uncle shipped me up to Fergus Falls to start the *Fergus Falls Telegram*.

"He also shipped up a 'Minnesota Chief' printing press, which, turned by hand, worked on the general principle of a threshing machine and shook every building in the block when it was in action."

The people of Fergus Falls correctly perceived the reason for the newspaper's existence—as a campaign machine for Kindred—but incorrectly assumed it would quietly die after the election.

Following one of the bitterest political campaigns in the history of the state, Nelson defeated Kindred for the Congressional seat that fall, but the paper lived on with Smith B. Hall remaining as editor of the *Telegram* for another year-and-a-half.

The *Telegram* was eventually consolidated with another Fergus Falls newspaper, the *Evening Journal*, but by this time Smith B. Hall was in the Twin Cities. As editor of the *St. Paul Globe*, Harlan P. Hall had offered his nephew the choice of a position in St. Paul or the job of assistant to the *Globe's* city editor in Minneapolis where the newspaper conducted a branch office.

Smith opted for the latter and an entry in his diary indicated why. "Minneapolis is to be my home for a while, at least," he wrote in April of 1884. "I made up my mind after leaving the depot and taking one look at Nicollet Avenue. I saw two runaways and one dogfight at the same time, indicating that this is a live town.

"I like a town where the people get on the streets and this town of Minneapolis suits me in this respect. St. Paul streets are like alleys to a fellow who has been used to Pennsylvania Avenue in Washington."

Smith B. Hall was to chronicle the growth of the city of Minneapolis, first with the *Globe*, and then, after his uncle sold that paper, as city editor for the *Minneapolis Times*.

After ten years in Minneapolis, Smith left to become associate editor of the *Kansas City Globe*. His duties with this newspaper included that of drama critic, and it was in this position that he met Mary deLuce White. Despite an 18-year difference in age, Smith began courting the young actress and, soon after, asked her to marry him.

"To the young stage-struck girl he fulfilled all the

requirements of belonging to a fascinating profession and looking the part," was how the courtship was described some years later in a Cincinnati newspaper. "To her inexperienced eyes, a nimbus of glamor surrounded her wooer.

"No doubt Mary White felt honored that this brilliant and distinguished looking man wanted to marry her. But worldly as he was, Smith Hall did not realize that he himself was at the deceptive zenith of his powers while the girl was just beginning to grow into the grace of mature womanhood. She was beautiful and would become still more beautiful. She showed signs of dramatic talent which might develop into genius."

Mary's dramatic ambitions in fact may have helped fuel the relationship, as some sources suggest that she was well aware of what an association with a prominent theater critic could mean for her career.

Regardless of who was pursuing whom, Smith B. Hall and Mary deLuce White were married September 24, 1895 at the Trinity Episcopal Church in Kansas City. Smith and Mary spent their honeymoon at the West Hotel in Minneapolis before returning to Mary's hometown.

But the newlyweds didn't reside long in Kansas City. Smith accepted a position with an eastern news service, and the couple moved to New York, where they lived at 79 W. 12th Street in lower Manhattan.

Mary continued to pursue her theatrical ambitions while Smith worked to secure her stage appearances. His endeavors on behalf of his wife's career were interrupted, however, when the news service sent him to Cuba following the explosion of the *U.S.S. Maine* in Havana harbor.

The events in the Caribbean were attracting worldwide attention, but Smith had other matters on his mind at this time. Back in New York, Mary was pregnant. So while the United States and Spain stood on the verge of war over the sovereignty of Cuba, Smith returned home in time to be with Mary on May 23, 1898 when she gave birth to Halsey Lewis Hall.

Although the name Halsey Hall was to become a familiar one to Upper Midwest sports fans, it was an appellation hardly recognizable to its possessor initially, as Halsey began his life answering to the family nickname of "Bundles." (Actually, his original name was not even Halsey. The name that appears on his birth certificate is Smith Lewis Hall. Apparently, sometime after his birth it was decided that he should have the first name of his grandfather, rather than his father.)

Bundles was born in Greenwich Village, but he and his family weren't destined for a lengthy stay in New York City. Soon after his birth, they were off to Kansas City where they moved in with Mary's mother, Effie White. However, these living arrangements also were short-lived, for it was during this period that Smith and Mary Hall separated.

By this time, much of the Hall clan was in Minnesota, congregated within a few blocks of one another in the Ramsey Hill neighborhood of St. Paul with many of them living under the same roof.

In 1900 they were joined by Smith and Bundles, who moved into a large residence at 102 Western Avenue North that already housed Smith's aunts, Harriet and Laura, as well as his father, Halsey R. W. Hall, and stepmother, Corinne Eugenia Campbell Hall.

Upon his return to Minnesota, Smith underwent a career shift, moving from newspaper work to public relations. He eventually owned his own publicity and promotion bureau in downtown Minneapolis.

Smith B. Hall, Halsey's father, was a well-known newspaper reporter and publicist in Minneapolis.

Halsey's mother, Mary, in 1903. By this time, Mary was estranged from Halsey's father and gaining notoriety as an actress.

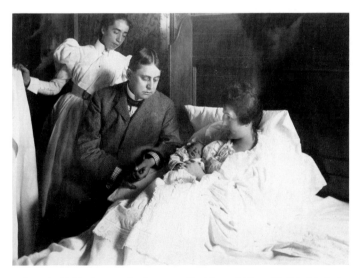

June 3, 1898: A nurse looks on as Smith and Mary Hall hold their 11-day-old son, Halsey.

Halsey, in January 1902, in front of one of
his favorite toys—a train.

Halsey with his grandfather and
namesake, Halsey R. W. Hall.

Relaxing on the front porch in the summer of 1907 are (from left to right)
Bart Gardner, Halsey's nine-year-old cousin; Halsey R. W. Hall; Gram;
cousin Jane Bacon (with doll); Smith B. Hall (in rocking chair); great
aunt Laura; and Halsey.

Father and son in May 1902   *Halsey in June 1904*

*Smith B. Hall at his publicity bureau in the Phoenix Building in
downtown Minneapolis.*

Halsey with his father and grandfather at Wonderland Amusement Park in June 1905.

The fabulous Wonderland Park was a favorite haunt of Halsey's as a youth. His early excursions to Wonderland helped foster a lifelong love of amusement parks.

Halsey's first residence in the Twin Cities was at 102 N. Western Avenue in the Ramsey Hill neighborhood of St. Paul.

The Hall family moved to this house at 3036 Portland Avenue in south Minneapolis in 1906.

Eighth-grade graduation from Madison School in 1912. Halsey has his chin directly over the "M" on the Madison pennant.

Halsey (back row, right) was the manager of the hockey team at Central High School.

Smith and Halsey on the latter's 16th birthday, May 23, 1914.

HALSEY HALL

"His heart is as far from study as Heaven is
from the earth."

Halsey's graduation picture in the 1916 <u>Centralian</u>.

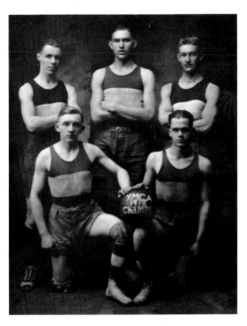

*Halsey (kneeling at right) played on a
championship YMCA basketball team in 1918.*

*Halsey was on active service in the
United States Navy from July 30, 1918
to September 18, 1919 and achieved the
rank of Yeoman Third Class.*

Smith became a press agent for traveling circuses, church conventions, and various political candidates, work which required extensive travel, mostly through the western United States. This itinerant lifestyle left him little time to spend with his son.

Bundles briefly was under the care of a nanny who reportedly induced drowsiness in him by giving him liberal whiffs of gas from the stove. From this, he developed rickets, a condition that left him with spindly legs. In later life, he joked about this characteristic (even calling himself "Birdlegs"), but he avoided shorts, preferring to keep his thin legs hidden with long pants.

The woman most responsible for raising Halsey, however, was his stepgrandmother, Corinne Hall, whom he called "Gram."

While Halsey grew up in relative comfort and was constantly surrounded by family members, he was not necessarily raised in an atmosphere of great affection. "From what I've heard of him, Smith was not a terribly affectionate type of father," said Halsey's daughter, Sue Kennedy. "And I found out for myself that Gram was also a cold fish.

"Gram lived with us when I was young. I remember Daddy once saying to her, 'Suzy's a nice girl, isn't she?' Gram replied, 'She's a very satisfactory child.'"

According to Sue, her father was quite different when it came to showing love, and she thinks his longing for it as a child may have been the cause. "He was a genuinely affectionate man and it may have been because of what he missed as a child. I think he was just starved for love."

Sue also reports that her father never even talked until he was four years old. "I was told that the first thing he ever said was 'Please hand me the shears.'

No one knew what he wanted to do with them, but those were his first words."

Even though he was seldom in town, Smith B. Hall stayed in touch with his son as often as possible and frequently wrote to him. One letter, written from Sioux City, Iowa in 1903, contains a series of alphabet poems which, according to Smith, "will afford all the mental discipline that your young mind should have. It doesn't have any pictures to illustrate it, but I guess you will understand it."

Some of the verses seem to indicate an attempt by Smith to maintain an influence in his son's upbringing:

F   *stands for fighting, although not a vice,*
       is generally spoken of as not very nice.

G   *stands for Gee-whiz, a very tough word,*
       and from good little boys it is never heard.

K   *is for kindergarten, a nice little school,*
       where Bundles is taught, so he won't be
       a fool.

X   *stands for "excuse me," and it's very polite*
       to say this when you don't do quite right.

Several of the verses relate to trains, a subject of fascination to Bundles:

C   *is for conductor who collects all the fares,*
       and sleeps standing up whenever he dares.

E   *is for engineer, a wonderful man,*
       and Bundles will be one as soon as he can.

U   is for Union Depot, where you see stran faces
    of people taking trains for many places.

The correspondence is signed, "Your misguided father, Smith B. Hall."

In 1904, the divorce of Halsey's parents became official. By this time, Mary's star was rising in the theatrical world and she was appearing in E. H. Sothern's "The Proud Prince" in Cincinnati. Even though she and Smith had already been separated for several years, newspapers across the country were more than happy to provide sensationalized accounts of the breakup of the marriage.

According to one story, "Mary went on stage with the understanding that she would only play in New York engagements, where they were residing. Her success, though, so aroused her ambition that theatrical life completely absorbed her.

"She began accepting traveling engagements, and Smith could not induce her to abandon the stage for a domestic life."

Another newspaper account reads, "Mr. Hall says that since his wife's rare brow has been clasped by the glowing diadem of success on the stage, she has deserted him.

"This cold wretchedness, walking a pallid specter beside the warm triumph won by Mary Hall in 'The Proud Prince' with Sothern, suggests a warning to all men who do not wish to marry until they are weary of the seductive frivolities and revolt against the keen excitements that youth longs for and maturity gags over."

There was no shortage of opinions from the tabloids regarding the reasons for the failed marriage, but a letter from Smith to Mary, written on *Minneapolis*

Times stationery and dated February 27, 1904, may shed a clearer light upon on the causes, as well as on their relationship, both with each other and with their son, herein referred to as "the boy":

> *Mary:*
>
> *Herewith find copy of decree granting divorce and giving me custody of the boy. I have not been able to ascertain just where you have been playing, owing to the change in Southern's (sic) bookings as published in the dramatic papers or I would have forwarded it before.*
>
> *The papers here have for a week past been getting queries from correspondents in Ohio cities who wanted to send stories of your prospective marriage with a "Cincinnati doctor," but did not use the stuff on my account. Had one of these stories appeared here the divorce would have been refused. I represented to the court that it was your devotion to the stage that separated us, and that there was no collusion for the purpose of enabling either of us to marry again. Your proposed marriage therefore does not place either of us in a good light, so I trust you will not have it exploited. There is even a law in this state which makes it a felony punishable by imprisonment for parties to a divorce to remarry inside of six months. The purpose of the law is to hold in check people who have no regard for the decencies of life, especially when the parentage of children is concerned. You assured me at Detroit in April that you did not desire to marry any man and I acted in perfect good faith.*
>
> *Pardon me if I do you an injustice, but your letter from Louisville and the newspaper lead me*

to conclude that the "doctor" story is true and the Cincinnati Post *a year ago told the truth, although you assured me at Detroit to the contrary.*

While you are nothing to me now and never will be again, I bear no malice and do not want you should suffer any more in the esteem of our friends than is possible. When you visit St. Paul and Minneapolis I trust you will be circumspect as your movements will be carefully watched.

During our separation I have been deaf to stories about you, have never allowed anyone to talk against you and have always sought to excuse your conduct on the ground of the "artistic temperament," even blinding myself to contain doings of yours which were not satisfactorily explained. Furthermore, I have always assumed more than my share of whatever fault there has been. I think this justifies me in asking that you do not make mis-statements concerning me for the purpose of justifying yourself. I don't fancy at all what you told others concerning me, especially you insisting that there was another woman in the case, which was absolute fiction, and you know it. Please try to treat whatever there has been between us with the dignity of silence. Remember that off the stage neither marriage nor divorce is regarded as a joke.

In view of your untimely "marriage" I want to ask two things of you: that when you come to St. Paul that you make no effort to see the boy—the less he knows about his mother now the better—and that as soon as you can do it conveniently and without injury to your prospects that you change your stage name.

Regardless of whatever assurances she may have made to Smith, Mary did wed Charles Tabb Pearce, the

"Cincinnati doctor," soon after. This union, however, proved no more permanent than her previous one. Mary was to marry five more times, the final one to Urbain Ledoux, an eccentric New York philanthropist known as "Mr. Zero."

Despite Smith's request, she retained the stage name of Mary Hall throughout her career. In addition, she did maintain some contact with her son. In 1915 Halsey visited his mother in New York and together they witnessed a performance by Enrico Caruso at the Metropolitan Opera House in the opera Martha, an event which Halsey later described as "one of the great thrills of my life."

"It was breathtaking," Halsey reminisced. "Caruso's voice was so perfect and true that tears came. When he finished singing, people were throwing their hats in the air, stomping their feet, clapping their hands, and shouting, 'Bravo!'"

Another visit with his mother in New York a few years later, however, may have left less fond memories. Dressed in his Navy uniform, Halsey was introduced by Mary as "her nephew" because she didn't want people to know she had a son old enough to be in the armed services.

Despite all he endured while growing up, Halsey was, on the surface at least, a happy child. He attended Maxfield School in St. Paul, only a block away from the house the family moved into on Rondo and St. Albans avenues. (They also lived briefly at 155 Nina, a half-block north of Summit Avenue.)

In 1906, the Halls—Smith, Halsey R. W., Gram, and Bundles—moved again, this time to 3036 Portland Avenue in Minneapolis in time for Halsey to begin third grade at Madison Elementary. One of Halsey's grade-school chums was Ed Ryan, who later became chief of police in Minneapolis and then served as Hennepin County Sheriff from 1946 to 1966.

Halsey played baseball in a vacant lot on 31st Street and 4th Avenue South and basketball at the YMCA. While he may not have been able to watch Halsey play as often as he might have liked, Smith undoubtedly was delighted at the interest his son was showing in sports.

In a May 1908 letter to Halsey (whom he still called Bundles even though he was now ten years old), Smith wrote, "I hope you have learned to play baseball better than the Minneapolis team does. Maybe I'll be home about July 1st to see how well you can catch and bat."

Despite the transient nature of his job, Smith tried to spend as much time as he could with Halsey. They attended Millers baseball games at Nicollet Park as well as vaudeville shows at the Unique Theater and the Pantages Theater on Hennepin Avenue. Smith served as the publicity agent for these theaters and would often let young Halsey write the reviews, which would appear in the *Minneapolis Tribune* the following morning.

Smith also handled the promotion for Wonderland Amusement Park, which stood on the corner of 31st Avenue and East Lake Street in Minneapolis from 1905 to 1914. The ten-acre park, which featured an enormous water slide that dropped 300 feet into a lagoon, and a 120-foot-tall tower with a searchlight that could be seen for miles, was a favorite attraction of Halsey's and helped to foster a lifelong love affair with amusement parks. He later was fond of taking his daughter and then his grandchildren to Excelsior Amusement Park on the shores of Lake Minnetonka.

Halsey attended Central High School, starting there in ninth grade when the school was still at Fourth

Avenue and 11th Street in downtown Minneapolis (in the building that later housed Vocational High School). His sophomore year at Central was the first for the school in its new home on the corner of Fourth Avenue and 34th Street South (the location it occupied until the school itself closed in 1982).

At Central, Halsey served as the manager for the hockey team and earned a letter in track and field by running the half mile. (His baseball career stayed confined to the sandlots.)

Halsey graduated from Central High School in June of 1916, and a line under his name for his senior class picture reads, "His heart is as far from study as Heaven is from the earth."

Even so, he apparently was a diligent student. At Gram's urging (or perhaps insistence), Halsey took summer courses in typing and bookkeeping at the Minneapolis Business College while still in high school. Upon graduation from Central, he enrolled at the University of Minnesota.

Halsey also worked as a stenographer for the Provident Life & Trust Company, which occupied suites in the McKnight Building in downtown Minneapolis. Next to the McKnight Building was an armed forces recruiting office which did a booming business upon the United States' entry into World War I on Good Friday in 1917. One afternoon the following year Halsey, instead of merely passing the recruiting station on his way to work, marched through its front door and enlisted in the United States Navy.

The war raged on, but the flow of U. S. doughboys overseas had ceased by the time Halsey was inducted into the Navy on July 30, 1918. So, instead of being stationed on a ship off the coast of France or England, he found himself in a recruiting office in Duluth, Minnesota.

At the time Halsey left for the service, few Halls remained in the Twin Cities. Halsey's great uncle Harlan had died in 1907 and his grandfather, Halsey R. W., followed in April of 1913 after a long illness that had left him confined to his bed for the final four years of his life.

Gram returned to Ohio in 1916 and on March 16, 1917 Halsey's father, Smith, died of pneumonia at the age of 58.

After returning from the Navy, Halsey did see his mother on a few occasions when she made stage appearances in the Twin Cities. Mary retired from the theater in 1929 and soon after married Urbain Ledoux, her final husband. When Ledoux died in 1941, Mary moved to Buenos Aires, Argentina and it was from here that she sent Halsey a postcard in 1945.

"Look me up some time," the message concluded. It was the last contact the mother and son ever had. In a 1976 interview with Irv Letofsky of the *Minneapolis Tribune,* Halsey said the last he knew of Mary she was still in South America.

Halsey went to his grave without knowing what happened to his mother. For the record, she did return to the United States and was a resident of the Village Nursing Home in New York City when she died December 8, 1960 at St. Vincent's Hospital, less than a block from the house in which she had given birth to Halsey 62 years before.

What makes a newspaper great?

"LOOK OUT, EMMA...YOUR BACKFIELD'S IN MOTION!"

How did the Golden Gophers' Bill Garnaas sneak in that winning dropkick in the 1942 Michigan game? Who played third base for the Minneapolis Millers ball club in 1916? What's the penalty for illegal checking against the boards in hockey?

If you want the answers (with personal demonstration where necessary) do what the Thursday Afternoon Ladies Sewing Circle does . . . or take a tip from inmates of Minnesota's Stillwater Prison. Ask Halsey Hall, sports writer of the Minneapolis Star and Tribune, and Little Giant Argument Settler for all sports fans of the Upper Midwest.

Mr. Hall is open for business 24 hours a day. At the drop of an invitation he'll address your luncheon club, church group or high school assembly on any sport from corn husking to World Series baseball. Or when the Cincinnati Reds' 1923 team batting average escapes your mind, give him a ring. Hall works and sleeps in installments punctuated by telephone calls from ever-loving admirers in search of obscure sports facts.

Halsey obligingly dredges up quick answers from his filing cabinet memory. He filters them through cigar smoke, and delivers them in a coffee-grinder baritone that's famous among radio listeners, who never miss Hall broadcasts of U of M football games (he's done them all since 1933 but one — when he was covering the World Series).

Even more famous is Halsey's fantastic irreverence for the English language in his Minneapolis Star and Tribune sports columns. From mere adjectives and adverbs he wrings the last ounce of color and pace. His on-the-spot stories, written in baseball dugouts, football locker rooms and hockey hangouts, are masterpieces of vivid word carpentry studded with sports oddities from his inventive, retentive mind.

"Holy Cow" (his favorite expletive) Hall is another of the genial newspaper personalities whose breezy writing, fresh talents and solid reporting abilities add new fun, new sparkle to life in the Upper Midwest, and whose work helps keep the Minneapolis Star and Tribune the best-read, best-liked newspapers of this great region.

Minneapolis
Star *and* Tribune

EVENING   MORNING & SUNDAY

More than 550,000 Sunday, 425,000 daily
JOHN COWLES, *President*

Halsey's sports expertise was enjoyed by a wide range of groups as shown in this November 1947 advertisement that the <u>Minneapolis Star and Tribune</u> placed in <u>Editor & Publisher</u> magazine.

Halsey the Writer

The First World War ended in November of 1918, but Halsey's military commitment was to last another ten months. On September 18, 1919 he returned to civilian life and immediately secured his first newspaper position, a reporting job within the sports department of the *Minneapolis Tribune*. In fact, so rapid was this transition that he didn't get a chance to shop for a civilian wardrobe before reporting to Fred Coburn and Charlie Johnson, his new bosses. As a result, Halsey spent his first night at the *Tribune* in his sailor's uniform.

Soon enough, however, he was outfitted in his familiar bow tie and striped shirt, and two months later his first byline appeared in the newspaper.

The event was the championship game of the state high-school football tournament, which was staged under the auspices of the University of Minnesota. Four finalists—Virginia, Worthington, Montevideo, and Bemidji—advanced to the semi-final round at Northrup Field in Minneapolis (the Minnesota Gophers' home field at that time).

Both semi-final games ended in ties. The school principals, concerned about how much class time the students would miss if the games were replayed, decided to let coin flips settle the issue and determine the entries in the championship game.

On Wednesday, November 27 Virginia and Montevideo, the winners of the coin tosses, squared off on the Northrup gridiron for the state title. Halsey was in the press box and the next day's *Tribune* reported the outcome:

Virginia a Winner Over Montevideo by 18 to 7

Range Team Wins Bitterly Contested Game in Race for State High School Football Title—Spectators See Splendid Fight Despite Cold — Rival Fullbacks Are Contest's Stars.

By Halsey Hall.

It required no toss of a coin to decide the winner of yesterday's state high school championship battle between Virginia and Montevideo, for Virginia broke the tie that binds in a most emphatic manner and ground the light but plucky Montevideo team into the sod at Northrop field by a score of 18 to 7.

Defense Forces Foe to Trick Plays.

Displaying an offense that could not be checked and a defense that forced their opponents to rely on trick plays to make headway, the lads from the North secured first rights on the state high school championship, while Montevideo, Worthington and Bemidji must be content with what honors they can glean from their tie contests in Wednesday's semi-final struggles.

For the next 41 years, Halsey's descriptive and highly colorful writing style was to be enjoyed by sports fans in both Minneapolis and St. Paul (and even across the country, as he also served as a correspondent for *The Sporting News*, a national sports weekly).

Halsey worked for a variety of newspapers and covered an even greater variety of assignments. Readers and colleagues remember his extensive newspaper career in many different ways.

"He was never a fan of the obvious," said Dick Gordon, who worked with Halsey at the *Minneapolis*

Star. "Once Halsey was taking a fishing report over the phone from our outdoor editor that began with 'As the sun rose in the east...' Halsey interrupted and said, 'Kid, if it rose in the west, you'd have a better story.'"

Gordon also remembered that Halsey was not the tidiest person in the world. "A building move by the *Star* sports department forced him to clean out his desk one day. Not since King Tut's tomb was opened was there so much dust. In one drawer he found a pair of socks as good as new and in another a two-year-old ham sandwich that wasn't."

Several of his colleagues commented on Halsey's rapid typing style. "Saturday mornings during World War II, he and I were the only two sports staff members on duty to put out the evening *Star,* but Halsey did 90 percent of the work," said Jimmy Byrne. "He was one of the fastest typists I ever saw in the newsroom."

"Because he composed the story in his head en route from the game site to the newspaper office, he could bang out his account in practically no time," said Glen Gaff. "He was an unusually rapid typist."

Tom Briere said Halsey was a "whiz on the typewriter," and that it was his custom to write the headline for his story before getting to the details. "One time he was about to send a page to be printed when he remembered that he had written nothing in the story concerning the headline. He had to rush in a last-second paragraph."

Halsey's assignments on the sports scene were varied. He went to wrestling matches ("This was before the days of stomping and kicking and stuff like that," he once said), took the bowling and golf scores, and for many years wrote a billiard column in the winter called "Cue Tips." (One of his favorite hobbies was billiards, and he won handicap tournaments in balk line and three cushion at Snyder's Recreation Hall in Minneapolis and at the Minneapolis Athletic Club.)

His newspaper work could include more than just sports, however. In a 1976 interview with Irv Letofsky of the *Minneapolis Tribune,* Halsey said on one occasion he covered a state cornhusking bee and, on another, a sewing bee at a downtown Minneapolis department store.

Sports were his main beat, though, and while he got to know many athletes during his years as a newspaper man, Halsey made a point of not socializing with them. "He always said that a writer should never get too close to the players because it could make it difficult in case he had to write something bad about them," said his daughter.

Rather, he hung out with his sportswriting cronies, especially Dick Cullum, Ed Shave, and George Edmond. He was particularly close to Cullum, who, following Halsey's death, frequently lobbied to have the new domed stadium in downtown Minneapolis named after him. (Cullum's campaign was unsuccessful; the stadium was instead named after another noted Minnesotan with similar initials—Hubert Humphrey.)

Halsey didn't stay long at his first sportswriting job. In 1922, he not only switched newspapers, but also cities, as he went from the *Minneapolis Tribune* to the *St. Paul Pioneer Press.*

Halsey was reportedly enticed into making the move by an offer to increase his weekly salary. Part of the lure, however, may have been the chance to cover the hockey team of the St. Paul Athletic Club (A. C.) that competed in the United States Amateur Hockey League and played its home games at the Hippodrome (now the Coliseum) on the State Fairgrounds.

"Down the ice in uncheckable rushes came the men

of the A. C.," penned Halsey in an early game account of this powerful aggregation, which was regarded as one of the top amateur squads in existence.

In fact, the first United States Olympic hockey team—which captured a silver medal in the 1920 games at Antwerp, Belgium—included three members of the St. Paul Athletic Club team: Eddie Fitzgerald, Tony Conroy, and Moose Goheen.

The 1922 A. C. squad that Halsey began covering had Fitzgerald as its coach and an array of stars such as Conroy at forward, Taffy Abel on defense, and Babe Elliott in goal. And then, of course, there was the great Goheen.

Francis X. (Moose) Goheen was an outstanding performer in many sports, but it was on the ice that he left his greatest legacy. Except for a period during World War I when he served in the Army, Moose played with the Athletic Club team (which later became known as the Saints) from 1915 through 1932. Goheen was eventually enshrined in the Hockey Hall of Fame in Toronto, the Minnesota Sports Hall of Fame, and the United States Hockey Hall of Fame.

Halsey was a great admirer of Goheen and, years later, recalled those days at the Hippodrome. "Nothing in sports could ever beat the sight of Moose Goheen taking the puck, circling behind his own net, and then taking off down that rink, leaping over sticks along the way."

In 1926 Halsey switched newspapers again as he returned to Minneapolis to join the *Journal*. By this time the balance of power in hockey also had shifted across the river. The Minneapolis Millers had lured Taffy Abel from St. Paul and brought in the legendary Ivan (Ching) Johnson from northern Minnesota's Mesabi Iron Range, additions that put the team on the

MEET THE MILLERS - - - 1937

TOP ROW—Stanley Spence, cf; Stewart Bowers, p; Belve Bean, p; Bill Butland, p; Reggie Grabowski, p; Jake Baker, p; Spencer Harris, of; Ralph (Red) Kress, inf.

MIDDLE ROW—Harry Taylor, inf; Fresco Thompson, inf. Jim Henry, p; Dusty Cooke, of; Carl Reynolds, of; Donie Bush, mgr; George (Skeets) Dickey, c.

FRONT ROW—(left to right)—Johnny Peacock, c; Walter Tauscher, p; Charley Wagner, p; Roy Pfleger, inf; Any Cohen, inf.

The Minneapolis Journal promoted Halsey's baseball coverage with this ad (although the Journal incorrectly spelled Millers' owner Mike Kelley's name).

verge of a dynasty.

The Millers' reign over the hockey world was brief, however, and came to an end when the National Hockey League expanded and formed a United States division. The new NHL entries raided the rosters of many Midwestern teams, a plundering that hit the Millers particularly hard.

While the ravaged Millers never completely recovered from this blow, Halsey remained an avid hockey fan for many years; in 1944 he was even elected president of the American Association of Hockey Writers.

At the *Minneapolis Journal,* Halsey's comrades in the sports department included Harry McKanna, Robert Edgren, Charles F. Knapp, Lester Will, Henry L. Farrell, and a boxing columnist who went by the nom de plume of Caully Flower. When Halsey joined the staff in 1926, the *Journal* sports editor was John F. McGovern, who had been an All-American quarterback for the Minnesota Gophers 17 years earlier.

Halsey's first year at the *Journal* was spent primarily covering college sports, but in 1927 he received the prime assignment as the beat writer for the Minneapolis Millers baseball team of the American Association, a Class Triple-A minor league only one step away from the majors.

Minor-league baseball and its operations at this time were radically different from how they are today. Baseball in the Roaring Twenties had yet to establish its network of farm systems, in which the minor-league teams are owned or controlled by a major-league "parent."

This shift in control began the evolution that transformed the minor leagues into little more than a feeder system whose sole function was to develop talent to stock major-league rosters. But the minor leagues of the early 20th century were entities in their own rights. Players were locally controlled and often returned to the same city year after year, affording fans an opportunity to build a strong sense of loyalty and identification with them.

Except for a team from St. Paul that had a short-lived stay in the Union Association in 1884, Minnesota did not have major league baseball until the 1960s. In fact, from 1903 to 1952 the majors were limited to only ten cities in all of North America.

But the have-nots did not seem to feel as though they were missing out on anything. Fans in minor-league cities throughout the country were more than satisfied with the baseball provided by their teams.

This was also the case for Halsey, both as a baseball fan growing up, and later as a member of the working media covering the game in an official capacity.

He quickly became known among the press-box denizens of Nicollet Park for his peculiar superstitions, particularly the belief that he could incite Miller rallies by standing in certain places. On one occasion he elbowed his way through a crowded press box, exclaiming, "I've got to get to the other side. We need a double!"

He often roamed the roof of the press box, which offered a more panoramic view, and he could easily become so engrossed in the action that he would forget his fear of heights. To get a better look, sometimes he would lean so far over the edge that his colleagues feared for his safety.

Halsey probably could have been found on top of the press box during the Independence Day game with the St. Paul Saints in 1929. The rivalry between Minneapolis and St. Paul extended to the diamond at that time, and meetings between the Millers and Saints were always intense affairs.

With Nicollet Park and St. Paul's Lexington Park separated only by a seven-mile streetcar ride, it was an easy matter for the fans of one team to follow their heroes across the Mississippi River into enemy territory.

The highlights of the inter-city games each year were the holiday doubleheaders. On Decoration Day, the Fourth of July, and Labor Day the Millers and Saints would play a morning game at one ballpark and the afternoon contest at the other.

It didn't take long for fireworks to erupt at Nicollet Park on the Fourth of July in 1929. The Millers were at bat in the bottom of the third when Hugh McMullen grounded to Saints' first baseman Oscar Roettger, who flipped to pitcher Huck Betts covering the base.

As they simultaneously crossed the bag, McMullen spiked Betts, who responded by firing the baseball at Hughie's head. Betts' throw missed, but Sammy Bohne didn't. Bohne, a reserve infielder for the Millers who was coaching first at the time, charged out of the coaching box in pursuit of Betts as the dugouts emptied.

George Barton of the *Minneapolis Tribune* called it "the most vicious affair ever witnessed at Nicollet Park" and claimed that it required "fully a dozen police to quell the disturbance."

Barton was the region's most noted boxing reporter, but it was Halsey who provided the most detailed blow-by-blow account of this fracas:

> Mc Mullen grounded out, Roettger to Betts who covered first. McMullen stepped on Betts' foot. Betts took the little white pellet and fired it hard at McMullen's neck. Bohne landed a right to Betts' jaw, ground-

ing him. Roettger rushed Bohne. Bohne landed a left and right on Roettger's face and the playing reserves arrived. Griffin cut Roettger's left eye and Bohne landed two more. Bagwell led the interference, was grounded and kicked in the eye, the optic swelled. Fenner rushed Bohne to the stands and Sammy sparred for space. The cops charged in, pulling right and left. They pried Bagwell off the ground. A few private fights started but the crowd was watching Bohne, and Sam gave them their money's worth. Campbell and Bohne mixed near the stands. Griffin landed a right to Van Atta's jaw but never phased him and the St. Paul pitcher charged. Bruno Haas came running in to remonstrate with the cops who were taking Campbell away. Wingfield broke in and battled with Campbell. Three cops took Campbell away while listening to Haas' impassioned oratory. Roettger walked to the bench, his eye a messy sight. Betts, Bohne and Roettger excused for the day. Much hubbub in the stands. Batboys peaceful.

The headline over Halsey's story the next day read "Sammy Bohne Doesn't Play, But Gets More Hits Than Those Who Do."

Three months later Halsey covered his first World Series, a matchup between the Philadelphia Athletics and Chicago Cubs that produced a pair of memorable events.

One highlight, which occurred in Game Four, was an

incredible rally by the A's in which they scored ten runs in the last of the seventh inning to wipe out an 8-0 Chicago lead.

"It was unbelievable watching all those runners pouring across home plate," said Halsey. "It looked like the Athletics were completely out of the ball game. Instead they set a World Series record for the most runs and hits in an inning, and won the game.

"It was one of those things you had to see to really appreciate."

While Halsey certainly did appreciate this game (he even called it one of his "biggest sports thrills ever"), it was the series opener that provided him with his first national recognition.

The first game of the 1929 World Series is remembered for Philadelphia manager Connie Mack's peculiar choice of a starting pitcher. Most expected Mack to open with 24-game winner George Earnshaw or Lefty Grove, who had won 20 games while leading the American League in earned-run average. Instead, he opted for aging right-hander Howard Ehmke, who had pitched only 54 innings all season.

In a 1974 interview with Patrick Reusse of the *St. Paul Pioneer Press,* Halsey recalled the reaction of his newspaper brethren at the site of Ehmke loosening up in the Philadelphia bullpen before the game: "Everyone though Grove was warming up under the stands and Ehmke was just a decoy.

"When the game started and Ehmke took the mound, someone in the press box said, 'The gamblers have gotten to Connie. The only honest sports left are wrestling and horse racing!'"

But Ehmke crossed up the Cubs with his slow curves and other off-speed offerings. He hurled a six-hitter and not only won the game, 3-1, but also struck out 13

Chicago batters to set a new World Series record. Ehmke's outstanding performance provided Halsey with a rich source of material for his first World Series story:

Chicago, Oct. 9—It is reported that Abraham Lincoln, once the manager of the United States, was told that General Grant had been drinking and Abraham Lincoln said, "Find out what he drinks and give it to the rest of my generals."

Wherefore, we find today the unusual situation in which Howard Ehmke, a pitcher who has been disciplined by Connie Mack for being a trouble maker and disturber and anything but a right sort of liver, is the hero of an opening World Series game. It is natural to suppose, therefore, that Mr. Mack now will insist all his pitchers become trouble makers and castoffs and then how will you stop the Athletics?

....As Ehmke went slow speed ahead to break Ed Walsh's strikeout record of 12 against the Cubs in 1906, he played no favorites. He fanned Cuyler twice and Hornsby twice and twice he got Hornsby, Wilson and Cuyler in a row.

Drama? Say, this old ball game was choking with it. Charley Root, pitching for the Cubs, was just as good as Ehmke, barring the strikeout touch, and for six innings Ehmke's slow curve and Root's sharp breaking wrinkle ball were masters of the day. It was a sight to see and the crowd was in frenzy as one batter after

another bit the dust and one fielder after
another came up with a sensational play....

Halsey's account of this game was included in a journal published annually at that time by the *New York Herald Tribune* to recognize the year's top sports reporting. He was to receive similar recognition in other national publications in the late 1940s and 1950s.

Most of his articles so honored were about World Series games, although one concerned the 1946 playoff between the Brooklyn Dodgers and St. Louis Cardinals for the National League pennant while another was a tongue-in-cheek piece on how to watch a football game. (Texts of these articles are included in the appendix.)

In 1932 Halsey had the opportunity to cover not one, but two World Series that were played simultaneously. The series between the Chicago Cubs and New York Yankees was the one most of the nation was watching.

Of equal interest to Minnesota residents, however, was the Junior World Series, a post-season contest between the champions of the American Association and International League that had been held off and on since 1903.

The combatants in the 1932 Junior World Series were the Minneapolis Millers, who had won their first American Association pennant since 1915, and the Newark Bears, who had won 109 games to capture the International League flag by 15 1/2 games.

Both World Series opened in the East, and Halsey stayed abreast of each by shuttling back and forth between Bears Stadium in Newark and Yankee Stadium in the Bronx.

The Millers-Bears series began Tuesday, September 27 with Don Brennan, a portly righthander known as the "Merry Mortician," holding Minneapolis to four hits as Newark took the opener, 11-0.

The next afternoon Halsey was at Yankee Stadium to see New York defeat the Cubs, 12-6; he then hustled back across the Hudson River in time for that evening's Junior Series game.

Halsey covered Game Two of the World Series on Thursday and Game Three of the Junior Series Friday before heading west as both series shifted locales.

The Millers held a two-game-to-one edge in their series as they boarded a train for home. Halsey rode with the Millers, but not all the way back to Minneapolis. When the train pulled into Chicago at noon on Saturday, Halsey hopped off and made a beeline for Wrigley Field where the Yankees and Cubs were preparing for their third game. He made it in time to witness one of the most legendary events in the history of the World Series.

The Yankees, already up by two games in the series, jumped out to a three-run lead in Game Three, but the Cubs tied it up in the bottom of the fourth.

With one out in the fifth, Babe Ruth stepped to the plate and, according to baseball lore that persists to this day, pointed toward center field before hitting a mammoth shot into the bleachers to untie the game. Lou Gehrig followed with another home run and the Yankees went on to win the game; the next afternoon they completed the series sweep.

Whether or not Ruth actually "called his shot" has been debated ever since. Halsey later said that Ruth "definitely indicated he was going to hit a home run on that pitch."

While his account of the game that appeared in the *Minneapolis Journal* the next day made no mention of any such indication, it is nonetheless clear that Halsey was impressed with the enormity of the Bambino's blast as he wrote, "It was an explosion that carried far, far out past the center-field side of the scoreboard in right center and, as the Babe circled around the precious sacks, the roars and boos mingled with cheers.

"So once again George Herman Ruth shoved it right down the Cub throats for he had been a target from the time the game opened. The Chicago bench rode him, the fans showered vocal razzberries upon him but the big Bam laughed and slugged, slugged and laughed. He had passed the sceptre to his understudy in brutality, Mr. Gehrig of Columbia, but he took it back again today."

Despite the drama provided by Ruth, the events of the New York-Chicago series could not compare with the bizarre scene that unfolded a few days later in the Junior World Series between the Millers and Bears.

The series was knotted at two games apiece, and the fifth game, at Nicollet Park, was also tied, 8-8, entering the ninth inning.

Newark had put runners at first and third with two out, when Johnny Neun hit a sinking liner into short left-center field. Harry Rice, the Millers' center fielder, dived for the ball and appeared to have snatched it before it hit the ground.

Both the second- and third-base umpires signaled out, bringing a group of charging Bears, led by manager Al Mamaux, out of the Newark dugout. After listening to the arguments, the four umpires huddled and reversed their decision, ruling that Rice had not cleanly caught the ball, thus allowing the go-ahead run to count.

Out came Millers' skipper Donie Bush, demanding an explanation. Again the arbiters called an impromptu conference, and again they came out with a different decision, reinstating their original call that Rice had made the catch. This, of course, resulted in an encore appearance from Mamaux.

The scene continued—the men in blue listening to the remonstrations of the offended manager, then meeting and emerging from their convocation with a decision reversing their previous one—until they had overturned their original call five times.

The Millers came out on the short end of the "Play of Six Decisions," and Halsey led his article on the game with "Minneapolis fandom has a hangover today from sitting in on a debauch of baseball inefficiency."

Of the rhubarb, he added, "The sum and substance of it is that nobody saw the ball on the ground. Therefore, justice rises up to ask, why is the decision reversed purely on circumstantial evidence when it would have raised no more havoc to have stuck to the guns that were fired in the first place?"

The next day, Newark rallied for three runs in the top of the ninth to win the game, 8-7, and the Junior World Series, four games to two.

While many in the Minneapolis media were quick to blame the umpires for the Millers' demise, Halsey passed on the opportunity and instead praised the victors:

"A rousing toast to the Newark Bears. A tribute to this flaming youth outfit of glorified speedsters with their college spirit, their heads-up baseball, and their splendid balance."

Halsey became recognized as one of the most knowledgeable baseball writers in the region. In 1934 he was elected president of the American Association of Baseball Writers, succeeding Bruce Dudley of the *Louisville Courier-Journal*.

Dudley eventually became league president of the American Association and Halsey found himself up for this post in 1946. He was one of a half-dozen candidates to succeed Roy Hamey, who had resigned to become general manager of the Pittsburgh Pirates.

The job went instead to Frank Lane, but a few years later Halsey was tapped by major-league baseball commissioner Happy Chandler to be a charter member of the Baseball Scoring Rules Committee, which wrote and reviewed the rules under which the game is played, and was re-appointed each year by Chandler and his successors.

Besides his reporting on particular teams or specific events, Halsey also wrote a regular column that appeared in whichever newspaper he was working for at the time.

His two longest-running columns, "Here's How" and "It's a Fact," included regular characters and features such as Simple Suzie, Neuritis J. Bile, the Barbershop Chord, and Do You Remember?

Neuritis J. Bile was a curmudgeonly alter ego who regularly expounded opinions usually unrelated to the world of sports—or anything else for that matter. A sample from one column in October 1929:

NEURITIS J. BILE coughed explosively into his cup. Then he blurted—"I would like to go out sometime in a congenial company where everyone wants to go to the same show. I have been invited to a dinner and the movies and a dance and vaudeville and the stock company and a hockey game in one and the same night and I should like to ask how a guy with only normal equipment can fill all these engagements at once..."

Simple Suzie was used as a lead-in for a play on words each day: "Simple Suzie supposes football players sleep under a nice light quilt made out of touchdown" or "Simple Suzie is doing her canning now and says she's made some delicious traffic jam."

His "Here's How" column also contained "The barbershop chord for today...", which ranged from paraphrased aphorisms to homespun philosophy. A few examples:

> —You can lead a pitcher to the shower water, but you cannot make him think.
> —The rooters hollered "Stonewall" and the line fell down like a ton of brick.
> —Do you manage the Cardinals or have you got a job?

For many years, his column concluded with the nostalgic "Do You Remember?" feature, in which he printed recollections from his readers (always crediting the contributor) of events and places from an earlier era, to wit:

> Do You Remember the time—
> ...when (going back is Burt E. Hallquist) kids went swimming in the raw at the creek where the Glenwood Chalet now stands?
> ...when (old time a-hunting goes Ed Murphy of the Soo Line) you opened a bottle of pop by giving the cap a resounding smack to release it?
> ...when (help arrives from Howard Ries, the Shakopee bottling gentleman) there was a horse trough at Broadway and James avenue N.?

...when (thanks to E. W. Evenson)
women wore black sateen underthings?

The observations he made in his column were sometimes sarcastic and biting, often humorous, and, on occasion, even downright poetic.

When Joe Louis scored a first-round knockout of Germany's Max Schmeling—who had become an unwilling symbol of the so-called Aryan supremacy—in June of 1938, Halsey opened his "It's a Fact" column the next day with "Heil, little ADOLF! And how are you?...That shower of small particles in Berlin this morning was merely ADOLF's moustache popping out, hair by hair..."

In April of 1929, Halsey was referee of a high-school basketball game between De La Salle of Minneapolis and St. Mel of Chicago. The Chicago squad came from behind with a furious fourth-quarter rally to defeat De La Salle, and Halsey's next column contained a wry reference to the game: "St. Mel did more shooting in the last quarter than the leading citizens of its community."

On November 9, 1940 the Minnesota Gophers beat the Michigan Wolverines, 7-6, on an 80-yard touchdown run by Bruce Smith across the muddy Memorial Stadium gridiron. The game was played in a steady drizzle that developed into a heavier rain. The rain continued and, two days later, turned into the Armistice Day blizzard that dropped more than 16 inches of snow on the Twin Cities and paralyzed the region. To commemorate the events, Halsey weaved a poem into his November 12 column:

> " 'Twas Showers that beat us,"
> The Wolverines say;
> But what if the athletes
> Had played yesterday?

47

At times, Halsey even doubled as a photographer, although he altered his name slightly when assuming this role. A picture of the Millers' Danny Taylor sliding home during a spring-training game in Daytona Beach appeared on the front page of the *Journal's* Sunday sports section on March 20, 1938. Under the caption was the credit line: "Photo by *Journal* staff photographer, H. Lewis Hall."

On August 1, 1939 the *Journal* was purchased by the *Minneapolis Star*, the city's other evening daily. Sue Kennedy recalled her father arriving home with the news of the consolidation. "My first question to him was, 'Will I still be able to read Dick Tracy?'

"It was one of the very few times Daddy ever got mad at me. He thought I should be more concerned with whether or not he would still have a job than if I'd still be able to read my favorite comic strip."

Halsey did still have a job (and Sue still got to read Dick Tracy). Both continued to be institutions in the new *Minneapolis Star-Journal*. One of Halsey's coworkers, Eddie Brietz, commented on how smoothly he handled the transition. "Halsey Hall didn't miss a comma when the *Minneapolis Star* annexed him and the *Journal*.

"He started a column in the *Journal* building and finished it in the *Star's.*"

Halsey retained his "It's a Fact" column and continued most of his regular duties, including his coverage of the Minneapolis Millers, at the new paper. With the merger, Halsey was reunited with his original boss in the newspaper business, Charlie Johnson, who had been sports editor for the *Star* since 1922 and who continued in that role with the *Star-Journal*.

Halsey's relationship with Johnson had always been an amicable one, and the two often enjoyed ribbing one another, both in the sports room and in public. Johnson once introduced Halsey at a sports banquet and used it as an opportunity to poke some good-natured fun at him.

But Halsey got the last laugh when he took the microphone. "Thanks a lot, Johnson. Let's you and I play horsey. I'll be the head and you be your natural charming self."

In 1941 another realignment of the city's newspapers took place with the purchase of the *Star-Journal* by the *Minneapolis Morning Tribune*. Both newspapers (the *Tribune* and the *Star*, which finally dropped the *Journal* name from its masthead) continued to function as separate entities.

Eventually, Charlie Johnson was made executive sports editor of both the *Star* and the *Tribune*. Halsey remained an employee of the *Minneapolis Star*, although his stories would appear in both newspapers.

"On road trips, one man might write for both the evening and morning paper," explained fellow scribe Dick Gordon. "If the reporter was with the *Star*, for example, his byline would be in the *Star*. In the *Tribune*, it would say 'By Staff Writer' or 'By Special Correspondent.' They wouldn't use the same name in both papers."

Halsey, however, was the exception. His byline could be found in both the *Star* and *Tribune*. Another colleague, Jimmy Byrne, recalled this as an attempt by Johnson to bolster readership of the morning paper. "Charlie thought they could accomplish this by putting increased emphasis on baseball. Halsey had such a great reputation as a baseball writer that often Charlie would have him cover the games for the *Tribune* instead of the *Star*."

Indeed, any newspaper that had Halsey's services was eager to promote the fact.

For example, a full-page advertisement in the *Min-neapolis Journal* in May 1938 featured a bold headline reading:

Synonyms:
"Baseball"—"Halsey Hall"

This dean of baseball sportswriters is known wherever the game is played for his keen insight of players' strengths and weaknesses; for his unlimited knowledge of teams in all leagues; for his shrewd appreciation of the strategy of the game; for his numberless friends among players, managers and owners; for his vivid style and humor in his daily stories.

In 1947 the *Star* and *Tribune* purchased a full page in *Editor & Publisher* magazine to promote Halsey as the "Little Giant Argument Settler for all sports fans of the Upper Midwest."

Halsey is credited by many as being the reporter who alerted Twin Cities' fans about the arrival of a great new center fielder to the Millers' spring-training camp in March of 1951. Willie Mays reported to the Millers on March 16, and within a few days Halsey had devoted his entire "It's a Fact" column to the new sensation.

"You watch him run and throw and hit and you are on his side in a minute," he wrote. "Willie is lithe, beautifully muscled, just under six feet, weighs 170 pounds, and doesn't vary in his weight off and in season. Righthanded all the way, he has great power to right center and here the dear old memory of Nicollet's fences in that direction comes back."

"Halsey was normally not one to get over-excited

about players in spring training, but he just went bananas about Willie," said Byrne. "I arrived in Florida a couple of days after Mays had joined the team. When I got to the ballpark and saw Halsey I expected him to ask how my trip was or at least say 'Hello.'

"But the first words out of his mouth were 'Wait until you see Willie Mays.' There was a cocktail party later in the afternoon and all Halsey could talk about was Willie Mays, Willie Mays, Willie Mays.

"In the next few days, I got to know what he was talking about."

Alas, Willie's stay with the Minneapolis Millers was to be a brief one.

Less than a month into the regular season, he was called up by the New York Giants, who by now owned the Millers, and Minneapolis fans saw their new hero disappear before most even had the chance to get out to Nicollet Park to see him play. His statistics with the Millers make it obvious why the Giants couldn't wait: a .477 batting average, eight home runs, 30 runs batted in, and 38 runs scored in only 35 games. Even so, his departure shocked and outraged the locals, who had assumed Mays would be with them the entire year.

Most remembered when Ted Williams played for the Millers 13 years earlier. Williams was the property of the Boston Red Sox, but they passed on the option of calling him up during the season, even though he was compiling incredible statistics and led the league in a number of offensive categories in addition to winning the American Association Triple Crown. The fans, as well as Millers' manager Tommy Heath and general manager Rosy Ryan, figured incorrectly that this would be the situation with Mays.

Although Mays wasn't the first, he was the most significant player to be plucked in midseason by the parent Giants since they had purchased the Millers from longtime owner Mike Kelley in 1946.

It was this event, more than any other, that drove home to local fans the change taking place in the operation of the minor leagues and the relationship with their major-league parents.

Recalls of other Miller players followed, and, as usual, Halsey had the last word on the subject. "Let Rosy Ryan and Tommy Heath have the gold removed from their teeth and send it to the New York front office. They'll get it sooner or later anyway."

Mays was gone, but the Millers carried on for several more years, and fans continued to be enamored with Halsey's colorful narration of the games. A few samples:

On an eighth-inning rally featuring Ray Broome, Marv Blaylock, Ray Katt, and Ray Dandridge:

"The eighth was altogether jolly, what ho! Broome walked and Katt's double brought him over. Blaylock's single to center counted the big Pussy and Ray Dandridge's singleton let Marvin romp home."

On a fine mound performance turned in by slugger-turned-pitcher Jack Harshman:

"Harshman, with pitches carrying the relentless timing of a parking meter, was the winner."

On an August 1952 game at Nicollet Park that took only one hour, 26 minutes to play, and that featured five home runs by the Millers, the final shot by Ray Broome capping the team's scoring in the sixth:

"In a game as rapid as a Manville divorce, Minneapolis whippeted to its ninth-consecutive victory Tuesday, hammering Charleston to defeat, 7-2...

"The slug-for-the-circuit symphony being as pronounced as it was, Roy Broome tuned in during the sixth cadenza."

On a couple of less than sterling performances by the Millers:
"The Minneapolis Millers stood around on base longer than Martin Luther at the Lyceum Friday night and wound up losing to St. Paul, 6-2."

and

"Technically, it was *Minneapolis Star and Tribune* night at Nicollet Park Monday night but, as the Toledo Sox defeated the Millers, 12-6, it had all the appearance of Lakewood Cemetery night."

Since he was regarded as one of the great experts on the game, Halsey was often asked to pick his all-star baseball team. On these occasions, he would rattle off the names without hesitation: "First base, George Sisler; second base, Rogers Hornsby; shortstop, Honus Wagner; third base, Brooks Robinson; outfield, Babe Ruth, Tris Speaker, and Ty Cobb; catcher, Gabby Hartnett; right-handed pitcher, Walter Johnson; left-handed pitcher, Lefty Grove."

But Halsey was remembered even more for his "Celestial All-Star Team" an aggregation he would make reference to when writing of the passing of a former great. On August 16, 1948, he reported on the team's newest addition—Babe Ruth:
"There's a one-two, cleanup punch on the Celestial All Stars now.
"Once again George Herman (Babe) Ruth is hitting ahead of Lou Gehrig. With the passing of the Babe, this peerless tandem of batting torture is reunited in

pastures where all infields are green and from where they may look down upon current mortals weakly trying to emulate their feats...."

Joe Soucheray, who started his reporting career with the *Minneapolis Tribune* in 1973, never worked directly with Halsey, but said that he was influenced by his writing nonetheless. "I went through back issues of the papers, started reading Halsey's accounts of the game, and discovered many differences between his style and that of a modern sportswriter.

"He described the game and the plays, something that is no longer done. Today's sportswriters make the presumption that everyone has already seen the game on television and will devote their time to trying to get quotes from the players after the game.

"Quite often these quotes are meaningless. The time they wasted getting them could have been better spent coming up with a nice descriptive sentence of the way a shortstop started a double play.

"Halsey was a wonderful writer. He would describe beautifully what a certain player looked like when he caught a ball and how he threw it, or how the sun shadowed half the field—things that quite accurately left the reader with a sense of having been there.

"I then began to realize that this was the way I wanted to write sports."

The respect Halsey received as a journalist was not limited to his peers or the fans who read his columns and articles each day; it came also from those who were the subjects of his reporting.

"Never have I met a man in baseball that I loved more than Halsey Hall, God bless him," wrote Otto Denning, an outfielder for the Millers in the 1930s.

"We all loved to umpire in Minneapolis," commented Joe Rue, who worked games in the American Association for many years. "The newspapers were all decent to us and Halsey Hall stood out."

"He was a great friend and a great writer who never betrayed a confidence," added Rosy Ryan, who served as field manager and later as general manager for the Millers.

And Halsey was never one to turn his back on innovation, according to Angelo Giuliani, a St. Paul native who caught for the Millers and Saints as well as several major-league teams. Giuliani claims to have once given Halsey an assist in relaying his game account from Kansas City to Minneapolis.

"The Western Union operators were on strike," Giuliani recalled, "and Halsey was worried how his story would get back in time for the next day's edition."

But Giuliani, who has raised homing pigeons since 1927, came up with a solution. "I put one of my birds in a crate for Halsey, and he hauled it down to Kansas City. When he finished his story, he put it into the capsule attached to the bird's leg and let it go.

"As I recall, the pigeon delivered Halsey's story on time and he made his deadline."

What stood out most in the minds of many colleagues was Halsey's accommodating nature.

"I first met Halsey when I was a cub reporter for the *St. Paul Pioneer Press* in 1943," said Don Riley. "He was so nice to young reporters—always giving them encouragement, even those like me who worked for a rival newspaper. I'd be really thrilled when he'd tell me I had done a nice job. He was so approachable—probably the most approachable senior writer in the Twin Cities."

Halsey retained this quality long after he left the newspaper game. In the 1970s Riley hosted a nightly call-in sports show on WLOL Radio. "One night someone called in with a question about the Millers that no one knew the answer to. A few minutes later we got a call from Halsey.

"He was listening to the show while out for a drive. He got off the highway, found a phone, and called in with the answer. He was a wonderful guy."

Dave Moore, the longtime news anchor at WCCO Television, started a neighborhood newspaper with his boyhood friend Jack Garske when they were 13, and Halsey was even willing to write a guest column for it. "I first wrote to Halsey with a question three years before and had gotten an immediate reply," said Moore. "Here was this seasoned newspaper veteran taking the time to write to a ten-year old kid and then, a few years later, actually writing a column for our neighborhood newspaper.

"My memories of Halsey's kindness explain why letters I get from children today receive my immediate attention."

Bob Lundegaard started at the *Minneapolis Tribune* in 1958 and called Halsey "one of the kindest people I ever met. He treated me as one of the gang right from the start."

Lundegaard also recalled the sportive atmosphere at the newspaper while Halsey was there. "Once Halsey was sitting at his desk when a colleague at a nearby desk was giving someone a football score over the telephone. The final score of the game was nothing to nothing, but the person at the other end of the line apparently didn't understand because Halsey's colleague had to repeat the score a couple of times.

"After the third time Halsey heard him say, 'The final score was nothing to nothing,' Halsey barked out, 'Criminy, why don't you give him the score by quarters?'"

Halsey had fashioned quite a career in the newspaper business, but in 1960 a new opportunity beckoned. Major-league baseball was coming to the area in the form of the Minnesota Twins, and Halsey was selected as a member of the broadcast crew.

For many years he had juggled the dual jobs of newspaper reporter and radio announcer, but this time he would have to choose between the two.

The decision was not a difficult one—he opted for the broadcasting position with the Twins—but it was not made without a longing look back.

Halsey never did leave newspaper writing completely. Up until his death, he had articles and regular columns in a variety of publications, including the *Skyway News*, a newsletter for Midwest Federal Savings and Loan, and the *Minnesota Motorist,* a magazine published by the American Automobile Association of Minneapolis.

He also had a column in the *Minneapolis Daily Herald*, a short-lived newspaper started by Twin Cities advertising executive Maurice McCaffrey to fill a news and advertising void created when publication of the *Minneapolis Star* and *Minneapolis Tribune* was interrupted in the spring and summer of 1962 by a 16-week employee strike.

Sports historian George Rekela, a University of Minnesota student at the time, claims that Halsey's byline was the only thing that made the *Daily Herald* worth buying. "He would send back stories from his road trips with the Twins that were quite entertaining," recalls Rekela.

In Halsey's "Herald-O-Gram," he wrote of a tavern in Baltimore that found a creative way of displaying its opinion of Orioles' second baseman Marv Breeding:

"They had a big sign on the front of the bar which said, 'Next drink 40 cents if Gentile hits homer. Next drink 25 cents if Brooks Robinson hits one. Next drink one cent if Marv Breeding hits one'...That is Mr. Breeding's reputation as a slugger in his home town."

Another story dealt with an incident during a series with the Kansas City Athletics:

"When the Twins beat the Athletics recently because one big A's run was erased when Jerry Lumpe failed to score before a doubling-up putout at second base, manager Hank Bauer hit a new peak for pique. He was so sore he refused to ride back to the hotel in the team bus."

The *Minneapolis Daily Herald* ceased publication shortly after the strike at the *Star* and *Tribune* ended. However, the *Herald's* editor, Francis McGovern, then started a newspaper of his own, the *Minneapolis Daily American*, which also featured a column by Halsey for many years.

Halsey's last newspaper stint was with the *Twin Cities Free Press* in 1977, and he still ended his column with the "Do You Remember?" feature, although by this time his reminisces concerned events from the days when he first began writing a column.

A contemporary writer wanting to use this feature might appropriately conclude a column with:

"Do you remember the time when (thanks to Angelo Giuliani) Halsey Hall was a legend beyond his own time?"

Halsey the Announcer

In 1923, a group of bankers and businessmen in Shelby, Montana had an idea.

Hosting a title fight featuring heavyweight champion Jack Dempsey, they thought, would bring national prominence to this oil-rich town and create a land boom.

A challenger was found with no problem—Tommy Gibbons, a St. Paul boxer whose manager, Eddie Kane, told the Shelby group, "You get Dempsey there and Gibbons will fight him for nothing."

Dempsey's manager, Jack (Doc) Kearns, wasn't quite as easy. But the promoters agreed to Kearns' demand of a $300,000 guarantee to be paid in installments prior to the event, and the bout was scheduled for July 4, 1923, four years to the day Dempsey had won the title from Jess Willard.

A huge wooden amphitheater, covering six acres, was built into a hillside at the edge of town to hold the thousands of fight fans expected to descend on Shelby. But problems in meeting the payments to Dempsey led to uncertainty as to whether the match would actually materialize. In fact, when the final installment of $100,000 could not be produced, the fight was called off—fewer than 48 hours before it was to have taken place.

Kearns finally agreed to take the final payment from gate receipts at the time of the bout. The fight was on again, but not before many of the special trains, slated to bring in spectators from across the country, were cancelled.

As a result, when the opening bell sounded, fewer than one fourth of the seats in the outdoor arena were filled. Dempsey never did get all the money promised him, and Gibbons ended up with nothing from the purse, receiving only training expenses.

As for Shelby, the fiasco forced the failure of three of its banks and ultimately bankrupted the entire town.

There may actually have been more elbow room in the Shelby arena than on the corner of Fourth and Minnesota streets in downtown St. Paul, where a huge crowd gathered outside the *St. Paul Dispatch and Pioneer Press* building to hear news of the fight as the ringside reports came in over the Western Union wire. Because of the great interest locally in the fight, the *Pioneer Press* arranged to have one of its sportswriters, from a second-floor window, deliver a blow-by-blow account of the fight through a megaphone to the fans below.

Gibbons, who later served as Ramsey County Sheriff for 23 years, was an idol to the people of St. Paul who had followed his career—along with that of his brother, Phantom Mike Gibbons—for many years.

Although he had lost only once and never been knocked off his feet in 86 previous professional bouts, Tommy Gibbons was a heavy underdog in this fight, and most predicted a quick victory for Dempsey.

But Gibbons defied the experts and even managed to open a cut over the champ's right eye in the first round. As news spread throughout the city that Gibbons was still on his feet and giving Dempsey all he could handle, the throng thickened outside the newspaper building.

"Gibbons hooks a left to the head," the man with the megaphone announced as the crowd cheered, with many flinging straw hats in the air to punctuate their enthusiasm.

"Dempsey hooks a left to the stomach and Tommy clinches," the play-by-play continued. "Dempsey misses a left to the body and Gibbons pokes two lefts to the head.

"Gibbons dances away from Dempsey's leads. Dempsey drives a right to the body and a left to the jaw as Gibbons backs into the corner."

And so it went through fifteen rounds. Dempsey won the fight by a unanimous decision, but Gibbons was heralded for his performance.

Disappointed as they may have been by the outcome, the St. Paul fans still went home feeling fulfilled and proud of their hero for having gone the distance with Dempsey.

Most left, however, without realizing that they had just been witness to another historic event. Because for the man with the megaphone—Halsey Hall—this fight marked the beginning of a long and illustrious career in sports announcing.

"They looked for the guy with the loudest voice, so I stepped right in," he later said. "That was my beginning as a sportscaster."

And for more than a half century after, Halsey remained a familiar and reassuring voice to Minnesota listeners with his friendly delivery and infectious laugh that was once described in a *Sports Illustrated* article as "redolent of happy days at grandpa's house."

Soon after the Dempsey-Gibbons fight, Halsey took to announcing in a more conventional manner—over the broadcast airwaves, instead of out a second-floor window—with a Monday night sports roundup, "The Call of the North," on WCCO Radio.

WCCO wasn't the first radio station to broadcast in the state, but it quickly became the largest. Halsey joined with other popular personalities such as Earl Gammons, Cedric Adams, and Clellan Card to help WCCO establish a national reputation it enjoys to this day as one of the giants of the industry.

Holding down jobs at both a newspaper and a radio station may have been strenuous, but, according to his daughter, one of the reasons he did it was for the money. "People always thought that, as a newspaperman, he made a lot of money," said Sue Kennedy. "That really wasn't the case.

"That's why he had two jobs for all those years. It provided enough money for he and my mother to travel and for me to go to school."

But while financial considerations may have been the prime motivator for his moonlighting, Halsey's entry into broadcasting opened a whole new world for him as a media personality.

By the mid-1920s he was already well known for his newspaper work, but it wasn't until he began announcing sports on the radio that his popularity began to soar.

Tom Jardine, who worked with Halsey at the *Minneapolis Star* in the 1950s, compared Halsey with Cedric Adams, who also combined a career as a newspaper columnist with one in radio. "Like Cedric, Halsey got greater by going on to radio and eventually television."

Halsey's following grew quickly, and one of his early admirers eventually became a broadcasting legend in the area himself. "He was my idol," says Dave Moore, whose visage has appeared in living rooms throughout the region during his more than 40 years as a news anchorman for WCCO Television. "Professional speech clinicians have even told me they can detect a lilt of Halsey's voice in my delivery.

"That's not accidental. Halsey had a real influence on me."

Halsey combined his regular sports shows with play-by-play announcing for some of the local teams and, by the 1940s, was more deeply involved in radio broadcasting than in his newspaper work.

Just as he had with newspapers, Halsey moved back and forth between radio stations. In 1935, he left WCCO to take a sportscasting position with crosstown-rival KSTP.

Soon after, he almost left the area completely when he was offered a job with the NBC radio network. Despite a great deal of persuasion from the network, Halsey turned down the offer. The uncertain conditions caused by the Depression may have deterred him from venturing into the largely uncharted world of network broadcasting at that time. In addition, he enjoyed living in the Twin Cities and working as a sportswriter, two things he would have been forced to give up had he gone with NBC.

"He felt he would do better by staying in the Twin Cities," says his daughter. "I guess he decided he'd rather be a big fish in a little pond rather than the other way around."

It wasn't that the position with NBC was not prestigious or sought after by other outstanding candidates. After Halsey turned it down, the job went to Bill Stern, who soon gained a reputation as one of the top sportscasters in the nation.

Although Halsey remained in Minnesota, he was on the move again a few years later. On Decoration Day in 1944 he returned to WCCO and began a sports round-up show that aired at 10:25 each evening.

"He'd leave home every night at 9:30 to drive down to the station for that show," recalled Sue Kennedy. "He'd pick up the early edition of the next day's paper from a newsstand by the Minneapolis Athletic Club, circle some items of interest in the sports section, and that would become his show.

"Then he'd hop back in the car and be home by 11:00. Mother and dad did a lot of entertaining, and that five-minute show caused him to miss at least an hour-and-a-half of every party."

Halsey shared the half-hour block from 10:00 to 10:30 with Cedric Adams, who read the news for the first 15 minutes, and E. W. Ziebarth, a dean at the University of Minnesota who hosted an international-news analysis program immediately prior to Halsey's show.

So popular was the trio, that when their segment ended at 10:30 each night, airline pilots would report seeing the lights in homes darken in droves throughout WCCO's listening area.

Ziebarth, however, declines to share credit for the number of listeners the station had during this time period. "The executives at the station reminded me often not to get a big head over the high ratings my program had.

"They would say 'How could you possibly lose when you come between Cedric Adams and Halsey Hall?' They were right.

"Maybe people were actually interested in international affairs, but I think my ratings were just a lucky accident."

Roger Erickson, who has since become a staple for early-morning listeners of WCCO, was the evening announcer when he joined the station in 1959 with duties that included introductions for the various shows and personalities.

"I was excited, yet nervous, about introducing Halsey for the first time," he recalls. "But Halsey made me feel at home right away."

"'Are you the new guy?', he asked me. 'Listen, when you introduce me, don't call me the dean of Northwest sportscasters. I know that's what the script says, but it makes me feel so old.'"

Halsey may have read scores and results from a newspaper or teletype, but his enormous knowledge of sports also allowed him to expound at length on the subject without any notes.

Erickson remembers a time that Halsey's show ran 15 minutes instead of the customary five minutes. "The problem was that no one told him about this in advance. As he's starting to wind up his program, he sees the director giving him the signal to stretch it out.

"Halsey had to go another ten minutes with nary a note, but it was no problem for him. He'd say, 'Pittsburgh won tonight, 3-2...and who could forget that great Pirate shortstop, Honus Wagner?' Then he'd fill some time with a story about Wagner."

Erickson reports another occasion that Halsey was forced to continue longer than he had planned. As he waited in vain for the wrap-up cue from the director, he finally barked, "What do you have there? A stopwatch or a calendar?"

Halsey was masterful at speaking off the cuff and, in fact, sometimes preferred to conduct his shows in this manner. When a Federal Communications Commission decree in the 1960s required that a script of some sort be used, however, Halsey merely scribbled notes on a piece of paper and read from it. A framed original of one such script, from a 25-minute sports broadcast he performed on WCCO in 1966, now hangs in his daughter's apartment in Tampa, Florida.

A few names on the large sheet of paper can be deciphered—Durocher, Koufax, Stanky, Mays—but most of the entries were scrawled in such an illegible fashion that they remained mysteries to all but the man who wrote them.

Before it was given to Sue Kennedy, the script occupied a spot for many years on the wall of a conference room at WCCO and was a source of great interest to the station's announcers and visitors.

It was in 1934 that Halsey hitched his wagon to a couple of rising stars when he began doing the play-by-play announcing for Minneapolis Millers baseball and Minnesota Gophers football.

This, of course, was not his first exposure to the Millers. In addition to his coverage of the team for the newspaper, Halsey had been doing pre-game broadcasts since 1932.

He got the regular announcing job two years later at the time when interest in the Millers was high. Led by the slugging of first baseman Joe "Unser Choe" Hauser, the team was in the midst of a four-year stretch in which they won three American Association pennants.

Halsey had plenty of opportunities to holler "Holy Cow!" over the heroics of Unser Choe (a German expression meaning "Our Joe" and the nickname given to Hauser many years before while he was playing in his hometown of Milwaukee). In 1933, Hauser had set a professional baseball record by hitting 69 home runs, and, in Halsey's first year as the Millers' play-by-play announcer, Joe appeared on the verge of rewriting the record books again.

Hauser hit 17 home runs in the team's first 20 games of 1934, but saw his season—along with his shot at another record—end when he broke a kneecap in July. The Millers had plenty more in their arsenal and, even without Hauser, still managed to win the pennant that season.

Through it all, Halsey didn't miss a pitch as he related the exploits of the team and the excitement of the pennant chase to thousands of listeners. "He could really bring a game alive in the days before television," recalled Fred Souba, a fan from that era. "With the team doing so well and with Halsey at the microphone, it was a great time to be following the Millers."

Halsey called the home games from his familiar perch in the press box at Nicollet Park. For several years, though, when the Millers went on the road, Halsey moved into the WCCO radio studio and, much as he had done with the Gibbons-Dempsey fight years earlier, re-created the action from the Western Union ticker.

"A recording of a stadium crowd would murmur in the background, its volume rising or fading to accommodate the changing action of play as Halsey described it," recalled Dave Moore in his book, *A Member of the Family.* "Behind Halsey's voice, a make-shift sound effects gadget created the sound of bat meeting ball. In later years, first Dick Enroth and then Ray Christensen would hone and perfect the magic to an even more polished state than Halsey had.

"But Halsey was the only practitioner at the time and he was wondrous! He put you right there in that game!"

As part of his duties as the Millers' announcer, Halsey became the spokesman for Wheaties breakfast cereal. It was at this time that Wheaties—which is produced by the Minneapolis-based General Mills Company—began its long association with sports by contracting for sponsorship of the Millers games on WCCO. In addition to the talent fee he received for reading the Wheaties commercials between innings, Halsey was also given more boxes of the cereal than he could ever hope to consume in a lifetime.

"During the years he was broadcasting the Millers,"

says his daughter, "there were boxes of Wheaties all over the house."

As immensely popular as Halsey was with baseball fans, the feeling was not shared by Mike Kelley, the Millers' owner, who thought that radio broadcasts of the games would deter fans from coming to the park.

"Kelley was convinced that the only reason radio had been invented was that God hated baseball and wanted to destroy it," said Jack Horner, who broadcast Millers' games in the 1940s.

"Why should I give my show away?" Kelley once asked, referring to radio. "If people want to know how we're doing, let them come and buy tickets."

"Kelley had an unusual way of classifying newspaper reporters," said Dick Cullum. "He rewarded his favorites by assigning them handles for his coffin.

"The most favored writer got the right front handle. The left rear handle was the least favored, but still a position of honor. Like the rest of us, Halsey moved from place to place on that coffin—until he went into radio broadcasting in addition to his writing. That infuriated Kelley to the point that Halsey lost his handle and never got it back."

The Millers were not the only championship team Halsey hooked on with in 1934. At the conclusion of the baseball season that fall, Halsey made his debut as an announcer for Minnesota Gophers football.

In their third season under Head Coach Bernie Bierman, the Gophers were beginning an unprecedented run of three consecutive national championships. Led by the likes of All-Americans Pug Lund, Butch Larson, Bill Bevan, Bud Wilkinson, Ed Widseth, Ray King, and Andy Uram, in addition to Babe LeVoir, Stan Kostka, Sheldon Beise, Phil Bengtson, Rudy Gmitro, and Julius Alphonse, the Gophers lost only one of 24 games and outscored their opponents 667-116 during this three-year stretch.

In 1934 Bierman clad his warriors in gold uniforms, and it was Halsey who first dubbed the team with the nickname "Golden Gophers." In these golden years, great excitement could be found even in a one-yard gain, according to Don Grawert, who described a typical play call by Halsey:

"Gophers ball on their own 20—first and ten. Lund takes the snap and fakes to Kostka...he keeps it, he's sweeping his right end! He's got LeVoir and Alphonse out in front! One tackler hits him! He keeps on his feet! Holy Cow! Another tackler misses—he's still going! Another miss! Finally he's down under a swarm of Wolverines! Officials mark the ball at the 21. Second and nine."

Halsey's years behind the microphone calling the Gopher action extended through all four presidential terms of Franklin Roosevelt and the administrations of Harry Truman, Dwight Eisenhower, John Kennedy, Lyndon Johnson, and Richard Nixon.

In broadcasting the Gophers from 1934 through 1973 (missing only the 1972 season during that span), Halsey also witnessed the coaching tenures of Bernie Bierman, George Hauser (who took over the reins from 1942 to 1945 while Bierman was in the Marines), Wes Fesler, Murray Warmath, and Cal Stoll.

Until recently, Gopher football games were broadcast on many different radio stations (at one point, a total of seven stations carried the games simultaneously). Halsey covered the games on a variety of stations and with a variety of partners.

His original broadcast partner on WCCO was Rollie Johnson. By 1935, Halsey had moved to KSTP and had a new sidekick, Brooks Henderson. His final partner, while broadcasting the games in 1973 on WLOL, was Frank Buetel.

In between, his list of partners included Bill Bloedel, Paul Wann, Dick Enroth, Jack Horner, Stew MacPherson, Ray Christensen, as well as Babe LeVoir and Bernie Bierman.

"Halsey loved doing the Gopher games," said Larry Jagoe, who produced the games for WCCO for many years. "He'd arrive early with his lunch and was probably the first guy in the press box. He was there even before the teams got onto the field.

"For Halsey, it was a whole day affair. He was there from ten o'clock in the morning to six in the evening."

During the years Bierman coached the Gophers, Halsey was the co-host of the Bernie Bierman Show, which was sponsored by P. B. Juster, the clothier, every Sunday morning. One week Halsey arrived for the show wearing one black shoe and one brown shoe. When Bierman and Juster pointed out the disparate colors, Halsey quipped, "I've got a pair just like them at home under the bed."

Babe LeVoir recalls another occasion when Halsey was not at a loss for words. "It was after Bierman had finished coaching and was serving as a color analyst with Halsey. I was with them in the broadcast booth during a game against Iowa in Iowa City when it was pouring rain.

"The rear of the radio booth at Iowa consisted of a sheet of tin; the drumming of the rain was coming through on the broadcast. Then, at one point, Bernie stepped out of the booth to relieve himself. As the drumming suddenly picked up in tempo and volume, Halsey announced to the audience, 'Ladies and gentlemen, the rain has now turned to sleet!'"

So successful were the Gophers of the mid-1930s

that the local broadcasts were often picked up by the networks and aired nationally. As a result, Halsey's announcing could often be heard across the United States and into Canada.

The network hookups continued through 1936, during the time that the British Commonwealth of Nations was being rocked by news of the engagement of King Edward VIII of England to American divorcée Wallis Warfield Simpson, an affair that would eventually cause Edward to abdicate the throne.

But to Halsey the scandal was a source of amusement rather than shock, and, following a big Gopher running gain, he couldn't resist a snide reference to the romance. "My gosh," he blurted, "the line opened up a hole so big that Wallie and Edward could have gone through without any interference!"

The wisecrack, however, was not well taken by Canadian listeners, who flooded NBC with letters of complaint. "Some sportswriter in Montreal wanted to have me lynched," Halsey recalled later with a laugh.

Halsey's irreverent nature could manifest itself in other ways during the Gopher broadcasts. Many fans remember the manner in which he once described the attire of the Michigan Wolverines as they charged onto the gridiron for a game against the Gophers:

"Michigan comes onto the field in blue jerseys and maize pants...And how they got into Mae's pants, I'll never know."

In 1950 the Gophers traveled to Seattle for a game against the Washington Huskies in their newly remodeled stadium. The multi-million-dollar expansion of Husky Stadium included a new press box on the front edge of the upper tier—approximately 165 feet above the stadium floor.

"It was so high that you felt like a bombardier

down on the field," said Ray Christensen. "It was actually a pretty good vantage point for watching the game."

While many media members agreed with Christensen's assessment, the acrophobic Halsey did not.

At a dinner the night before the Washington-Minnesota game, Roy Stockton of the *Seattle Post* cautioned the visiting media to not make the same mistake Bill Stern had made the previous week when he said the press box was so high that he could see the Pacific Ocean.

"It was Lake Washington he was looking at," explained Stockton. "You cannot see the Pacific Ocean from there."

The next day a petrified Halsey recalled Stockton's advice as he entered the press box. As the broadcast opened he explained the new press accommodations to listeners. "We're so high up," he exclaimed, "I can see the Indian Ocean!"

Despite the occasional on-air antics, Halsey was regarded as a top-flight professional by his peers. In 1959 he was voted Sportscaster of the Year by the National Sportscasters and Sportswriters Association.

Paul Giel, a two-time Gopher All-American, recalled an incident that demonstrated Halsey's experience behind the microphone. Prior to becoming the University of Minnesota men's athletic director in 1972, Giel was the sports director for WCCO Radio and, as a result, was often in the broadcast booth with Halsey before and during games. "Once we were at Purdue getting ready to do the pre-game show," said Giel. "The producer hadn't yet arrived with the scripts for the show's commercials, and we were wondering what we were going to do."

"While the rest of us panicked, Halsey calmly got on the phone back to WCCO, asked who the sponsors were and for some information on each. We did the show with Halsey ad-libbing each of the commercials and doing as good a job as he would have had he had the script.

"He'd been through things like this before, and it didn't faze him at all. He was such a pro."

For several years, Halsey was a regular guest on the "Roundy Predicts" television show, hosted by Joseph (Roundy) Coughlin, a sports columnist for the *Wisconsin State Journal* in Madison. Coughlin, who gained a modicum of regional notoriety and became known as the "Great Prognosticator" in the mid-1950s after claiming to have correctly predicted the outcome of 52 consecutive college football games, had a television show in Madison as well as on WCCO in Minneapolis during the football season. Each week, Roundy traveled to the Twin Cities for his show in which he, helped by Halsey and other local sports personalities, predicted the results of the upcoming Big Ten games.

Giel, along with many others, commented on the great love Halsey had for the University of Minnesota and its athletic teams.

Halsey corresponded frequently with Marsh Ryman, who was athletic director for the University in the 1960s. Without fail, his letters to Ryman included greetings to the various Gopher coaches, such as Dick Siebert (baseball), John Kundla (basketball), Murray Warmath (football), Roy Griak (track and field), John Mariucci (hockey), as well as sports information director Otie Dypwick.

"He loved the Gophers so much that he seemed to resent the intrusion of the Minnesota Vikings," said his daughter, Sue. "He was never a big Vikings fan. He always thought they would interfere with the Gophers."

On several occasions, when the Gopher football team was experiencing difficult times, Halsey wrote letters of encouragement to the team captains, who read the letters to their teammates in the locker room before a game.

Here are excerpts from a letter that Halsey sent to Darrel Bunge and Jeff Gunderson in 1973 following losses to Ohio State, Kansas, and Nebraska: "You have faced some of the behemoths of football. You never quit...You have improved with every game, regardless of the score. I was proud of you at Columbus [Ohio], Lawrence [Kansas], and here [against Nebraska]. Keep your chin up, boys. Better times will come."

Better times did come for the Gophers. They beat Indiana, 24-3, and after the game, Coach Cal Stoll and several of the players commented on the inspirational effect Halsey's letter had had on the squad.

In appreciation for Halsey's years of broadcasts and support of the Gophers, the University of Minnesota "M" Club eventually awarded Halsey an honorary letterman's blanket.

With more than 30 years of broadcasting under his belt by 1960, Halsey had reached a point in his life that, for many people, would have brought about thoughts of retirement. For Halsey, though, a new career was about to begin.

On October 26, 1960 Calvin Griffith, owner of the Washington Senators, announced he was moving his baseball team to Minnesota for the 1961 season. Among the numerous tasks facing Griffith as he prepared to move an American League franchise halfway across the country was that of putting together a television and radio package for the team and selecting announcers for the games.

After agreements were reached for WCCO Radio and

WTCN Television to air the games, a pair of play-by-play announcers was decided upon. Bob Wolff, an announcer for the Senators since 1947, was retained and moved to Minnesota with the team, which would be known as the Minnesota Twins, while Ray Scott, best known as an announcer for the Green Bay Packers, was brought on board to join him.

The final spot on the broadcast team was that of color analyst, and many maintain that little suspense existed over who would fill that role.

Griffith, who participated in the selection of the announcers along with the sponsors and stations, said he had had Halsey in mind even before the actual decision to move the Senators to Minnesota had been finalized.

Griffith had first met Halsey in July of 1958 when the Senators played an exhibition game against the Philadelphia Phillies in Minnesota. "He interviewed me while I was in town," said Griffith. "When it was over, I thought 'This man is a master. He has a vocabulary as good as Mr. Churchill's and he knows how to use it.'

"When it came time to make a decision on the final member of the broadcast crew, I recommended Halsey. The fans loved him. He was a real hero to the people of this area. He was fantastic."

At the age of 62, Halsey Hall had made the majors.

"I remember the day he came to our house with the news that he'd been chosen to be a Twins' broadcaster," recalls Halsey's daughter. "He was thrilled to death on the one hand, but he also felt bad because it meant he would have to give up his job with the newspaper."

Despite the fact that it meant leaving the *Minneapolis Star,* Halsey characterized his selection as a member of the Twins' broadcast team as "the biggest break I ever got."

His early broadcast partners recall what it was like working with Halsey.

"Halsey was not your general run-of-the-mill sports-caster," said Wolff. "He was truly a man of the people, which added an element to the broadcasts that is rarely found.

"During the one year I was with the Twins, I was repeatedly amazed by all the people who made their pilgrimage to the radio booth at Met Stadium to see Halsey. It was something I had never before seen in all my years in broadcasting."

Ray Scott said he and Halsey developed an "instant rapport."

"With Halsey," added Scott, "what you see is what you get. He was such a kindly man; I never heard him speak ill of anyone. And it was obvious that he knew and loved the sport of baseball.

"Having Halsey in the booth was like having more than four decades of living baseball history at your fingertips."

While Halsey's years in writing and broadcasting had brought him numerous thrills, there were many great moments yet to be witnessed. A pair of events, in particular, stood out in his mind.

One took place April 11, 1961 at Yankee Stadium in New York as the Twins took on the defending American League champion New York Yankees in their first game. Whitey Ford, who went on to win 25 games that season, was on the mound for New York, but it was Pedro Ramos of the Twins who emerged on top in this contest, as he held the mighty Yankees to three hits while Bob Allison and Reno Bertoia homered to lead the Twins to a 6-0 victory in their initial opener.

Another big event came on September 25, 1965 as the Twins beat Washington, 2-1, to clinch the American League pennant. In addition to receiving an airplane spin courtesy of first baseman Don Mincher, Halsey ended up drenched with champagne as he ventured into the victorious locker room after the game to interview the new league champions. "I got about four bottles poured over my head and only two jiggers in my mouth," he later said of the celebration.

Twins' fans remember Halsey for a variety of traits during his years as an announcer for the team. Instead of signing off from a broadcast with "goodbye" or "goodnight", Halsey bade farewell in a foreign language, and, more often than not, "auf Wiedersehen" was what fans heard at the conclusion of the game.

The anxiety he experienceed in watching the end of exciting games was another Halsey hallmark. "There were times he was so afraid to watch that he practically had his eyes closed," said Scott. "Many a tight game ended with me saying, 'You can get up off the floor now, Halsey.'"

Halsey looked forward to many events each season, but Bat Day was not among them. Once a year, youngsters attending a Twins' game were presented with a new Louisville Slugger as they passed through the turnstiles. As the kids pounded their bats on the metal decking at Metropolitan Stadium throughout the game, Halsey would become increasingly concerned over the structural integrity of the ball park. "The broadcast booth at Met Stadium was located between the second and third decks," said Herb Carneal, who had taken over for Bob Wolff on the Twins' broadcast crew in 1962. "As the kids kept pounding those bats in unison, Halsey was sure the entire stadium was going to collapse.

"Halsey would then go into his best W. C. Fields'

77

impersonation and say, 'Why don't they get these juvenile delinquents out of here?'"

The din of the bats also created challenges in reading commercials between innings. One famous clip from the WCCO Radio archives features Halsey increasing the volume of his voice until he is actually shouting while reading the advertising copy for a sponsor.

Carneal also remembers Halsey for his love of green onions and cigars, a combination that created a certain degree of discomfort for his compatriots in the booth. "Halsey always loved a good cigar," joked Carneal. "Unfortunately, that wasn't the kind that he smoked."

"My wife was helping me unpack after a road trip once," said Ray Scott, "and she said, 'I thought you had quit smoking.' I had quit many years earlier, but it was difficult convincing her that I had not taken up the habit again.

"Every piece of clothing I had reeked of smoke, as well as the odor of onions."

The most-remembered incident involving Halsey's cigars took place during a game at Comiskey Park in Chicago in early June of 1968. Midway through the finale of a doubleheader between the Twins and White Sox, the ashes from Halsey's cigar ignited a large mass of ticker tape that had piled up on the press box floor in the course of the afternoon.

Smoke began drifting upward and Halsey turned to see his sport coat, which was draped over his chair, in flames. The fire was brought under control, but not before a large hole had been burned in his jacket.

News of the conflagration reached Minnesota and, when the Twins returned from their road trip, the 3M Company of St. Paul presented Halsey with an asbestos sports coat.

Twins' catcher Jerry Zimmerman quipped, "Halsey's

the only man I know who can turn a sports coat into a blazer."

Scott was gone from Twins' broadcasts by this time, but says the fire in Chicago was not the first ever started by Halsey and his cigar. "On more than one occasion, I found myself trying to call the action while flames were lapping at the cuffs of my pants.

"The funniest thing, though, was that when I would ask Halsey to be more careful with his cigar and matches, he would say, 'How did you know it was me?'

"In his own inimitable fashion, he would genuinely wonder why we were blaming him."

Stew MacPherson also recalled fires started by Halsey when the pair worked together on Gopher broadcasts years earlier. "He was a menace, albeit a lovable one," says MacPherson.

But Halsey had other idiosyncracies besides his penchant for pyromania.

His broadcasting career had begun before such technological advances as 'cough switches' allowed an announcer to deactivate a microphone momentarily by pushing a button or a switch. According to Scott, Halsey never did get accustomed to using such a device. "If he didn't want something going over the air, he would cover his microphone. The problem was Halsey thought that putting just one finger over the mike was enough to do the job and that no one would be able to hear him.

"On more than one occasion, a few comments that he didn't intend for public broadcast went over the air; fortunately, it was never anything too bad."

Herb Carneal was present for a reverse situation— when Halsey was trying to announce a game, but his words weren't making the airwaves. The reason was simple; Halsey was talking into a stopwatch instead of his microphone.

"It was during a spring-training game in Florida," explained Carneal. "For some reason, the engineer thought there would be only one announcer, so he had brought just one microphone on a stand. When he discovered he needed another one, he came up with a lavaliere microphone, which is to be clipped on the shirt.

"Halsey didn't feel like clipping it on since he got up and down and moved around so much in the booth. Instead, he just laid it on the counter and picked it up when he needed to talk into it.

"Suddenly the engineer is punching me and pointing at Halsey. I looked and saw that, instead of the microphone, Halsey had picked up a stopwatch and was talking into that."

Upon his discovery of the mistake, Halsey burst into uncontrollable fits of laughter while Carneal announced to listeners, "Halsey has just revolutionized radio."

Halsey and Herb were left in similar hysterics on another occasion, when Halsey suffered a mix-up in words as he tried to tell listeners about a promotion at the ball park that evening in which all women in attendance were given a free pair of pantyhose.

"In promotions here tonight, fans, it was *pantywaist* night."

Said Scott of his former colleague: "Halsey was a genius at directing attention toward himself when something went wrong. And when it happened, he was the one laughing louder than any of us."

From 1961 through 1972, Halsey was at every game played by the Minnesota Twins. During this stretch of nearly 2,000 games, he watched Jack Kralick and Dean Chance hurl no-hitters, Rod Carew and Tony Oliva win batting titles, Harmon Killebrew slug his way to five home-run crowns, and the Twins play in the 1965 World Series against the Los Angeles Dodgers.

For two years, in 1968 and 1969, Halsey also hosted a pre-game television show on WTCN. The 15-minute "Halsey Hall Show" featured notables from the game as well as fans, who had the chance to stump Halsey with a baseball question.

Following the 1972 season, however, the decision was made by WCCO Radio to remove Halsey from the broadcast team. The exact reasons were never made public, but most believed that the station, as well as the Twins, were concerned about the strenuous nature of the work and the effect it was having on Halsey, who was 74 by this time.

Halsey maintained he was still up to the rigors of the job, including the travel, but the decision was final.

The name Halsey Hall would, however, remain synonymous with the Minnesota Twins thanks to Hal Greenwood, president of Midwest Federal Savings and Loan, which was the prime sponsor of the team's broadcasts at this time.

Halsey was hired by Midwest Federal as an "Ambassador of Baseball," with duties that included presiding over Opening Day ceremonies for the Twins as well as rejoining the broadcast crew to do the announcing on selected home games.

Even though his voice and laugh were no longer regular features of Twins' broadcasts, he continued to receive as much fan mail as any sportscaster in the Twin Cities.

In a survey performed by the *Minneapolis Star* regarding television in the 1970s, Halsey was picked by readers as the area's top sportscaster, even though the poll was taken in 1979—two years after his death.

"He was the king of them all with the microphone,"

said Calvin Griffith. "He was the best there's ever been in Minnesota."

"The things I'll remember most about Halsey," added Ray Scott, "were his great zest for life and his incredible sense of humor. Along with this, though, came a great sense of fair play."

"He was a joy to work with," responded another former broadcast partner, Stew MacPherson. "With Halsey, you never knew what was going to happen next.

"It's been said that no one is irreplaceable. But Halsey, God bless him, destroyed that myth."

Sports announcers who "know their stuff" were selected to supply the play-by-play accounts of the 57 important college football games being broadcast this fall under the sponsorship of the Chevrolet Motor Company. In numerical order above are shown: (1) Bill Mundy, famous Atlanta Journal sports authority who broadcasts each week over WSB; (2) Neal Barrett, former football star, KOMA, Oklahoma City; (3) the WCCO (Minneapolis-St. Paul) staff, left to right, Jack Quinlan, Journal sports editor; Halsey Hall and Rollie Johnson; (4) Howard "Nig" Berry, former Pennsylvania and All-American fullback, WIP, Philadelphia; (5) Jack Ryan, of KYW, Chicago; (6) the famous Ty Tyson, of WWJ, Detroit; (7) Jerry Mann, All-American quarterback (Southern Methodist 1927); KTRH and Southwestern Network and (8) Bob Longstreet, of WXYZ and Michigan Network.

Regarded as one of the top college football announcers in the country, Halsey was featured in this collage of announcers for nationally broadcast games sponsored by the Chevrolet Motor Company.

Halsey's friendly delivery was once described in a <u>Sports Illustrated</u> article as "redolent of happy days at Grandpa's house."

Calling the action from the Memorial Stadium press box. Halsey did the play-by-play announcing for Gopher football for more than 40 years.

Along with Clellan Card and Dick Cullum, Halsey helps Roundy Coughlin analyze the just-completed 1964 Big Ten football season. Halsey was a regular on the "Roundy Predicts" show for many years.

Nicollet Park, the home of the Minneapolis Millers for 60 years, closed following the 1955 season. On September 25 of that year, Halsey hosted a pre-game ceremony to commemorate the final Sunday game to be played at Nicollet. Several Millers' stars from an earlier era were on hand for the event, which concluded with the burning of a Nicollet Park replica on the pitcher's mound.

The team of Ray Scott, Halsey Hall, and Herb Carneal brought Twins' action to Upper Midwest baseball fans during the 1960s.

Vice President Hubert Humphrey frequently visited Halsey in the broadcast booth at Met Stadium.

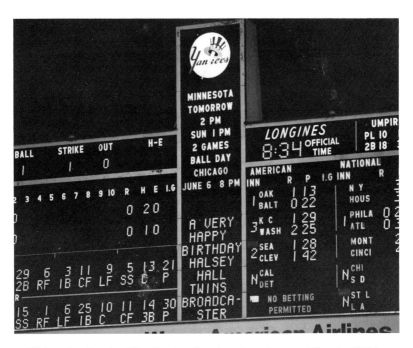

Halsey developed a following in other American League cities. In 1969 he received 400 birthday cards from fans in New York as well as this greeting on the Yankee Stadium scoreboard.

Twins' president Calvin Griffith and Halsey in 1961.

After starting a fire in the press box and burning his sport coat, Halsey was presented with an asbestos jacket from the 3M Company.

Halsey with Gopher athletic director Ike Armstrong, Connie Mack, and Bernie Bierman in November 1950. Mack had just stepped down as manager of the Philadelphia Athletics after 50 years in that post (he also owned the team, a fact that accounted for his longevity); Bierman had also just resigned as Gopher football coach.

Interviewing New York Giants' manager Leo Durocher during the <u>Minneapolis Star and Tribune</u> Parade of Champions dinner at the Nicollet Hotel in May 1950.

Halsey presides over a reunion of the 1934 Gophers, Bernie Bierman's first national championship team. Bierman is seated third from the left.

Cedric Adams looks on as Halsey addresses a group in Minneapolis. Hubert Humphrey once called Halsey "one of the few men who has given more speeches in Minnesota than I have."

Halsey the Speaker

Halsey Hall was at home with a microphone, not just in a broadcast booth or studio, but from behind a lectern as well.

In 1941, he delivered a speech at a high-school banquet in Anoka, Minnesota that blossomed into still another calling; within two decades he came to be regarded as the leading toastmaster in the Upper Midwest as he regaled hundreds of audiences as a speaker and as a master of ceremonies.

By the mid-1960s, Halsey was making more than 50 appearances a year on the dais and was once told by Hubert Humphrey, the former vice president of the United States and himself a prolific orator, "You are one of the few men in Minnesota who has made more speeches than I have."

"Facts, Fairness, and Fun" was Halsey's motto as a speaker. "Be sure of your facts, always be fair, and have fun—or get out of the business," he said often. It was a formula that worked well for him.

"He was second to none," said Norm McGrew, the former general manager of the Minneapolis Chamber of Commerce. "We used him all the time for dinners and other functions put on by the Chamber.

"And when other organizations asked us if we could recommend a speaker, we'd always give them Halsey's name. If he was the master of ceremonies for an event, you could be assured of a success."

Tom Jardine seconded the sentiments of McGrew. As a member of the promotions department for the *Minneapolis Star*, Jardine was involved in the formation of the Minnesota Sports Hall of Fame, which was created by the newspaper in 1958. "The banquet to induct the original members was quite an affair. We wanted to make sure everything was first class, so, of course, the first thing we did was line up Halsey to be the master of ceremonies."

So adeptly did Halsey perform his duties, which included interviewing the new inductees who were present, that Charlie Johnson wrote in his *Minneapolis Star* column the next day, "Guiding the whole show in his inimitable style was the last word in masters of ceremonies—Halsey Hall."

For years after, Halsey was asked back to preside over the annual induction ceremonies for the Minnesota Sports Hall of Fame. He also became the regular toastmaster for the Mid-Winter Baseball Banquet, which was sponsored each year by the Midwest Sportscasters Association.

"As a master of ceremonies, he was known for keeping a fast pace," said Halsey's daughter, Sue. "The program really moved when he was handling it."

Halsey was also remembered for his ability to assist speakers suffering from stagefright. Many of the speakers introduced by him were athletes who had routinely demonstrated great poise while performing before thousands of people on the field of play; yet for some, being called on to say a few words to an audience could cause unbearable anxiety.

In these cases, Halsey displayed an incredible knack for relaxing the speakers; if necessary, he would even stay at the microphone with the speaker to help him through the anxious moments.

His efforts in this role were recognized in 1957 when he was named "Outstanding Master of Ceremonies in the Twin Cities" by the Minneapolis Advertising Club.

Another tribute to Halsey's skills in this area was paid by American Association president Ed Doherty, who watched Halsey perform as master of ceremonies at a baseball banquet in Minneapolis. "In my estimation, Halsey, you are the world's greatest toastmaster," said Doherty, who backed up his words by inviting Halsey to his hometown of Louisville to preside over a similar affair there.

Sue Kennedy said that even though her father was often asked which he enjoyed more—being a speaker or being a master of ceremonies—he didn't have a preference. "He liked them both. He felt at home on stage no matter what he was doing."

In either role, he relied on and was well served by his spontaneous wit and extraordinary sense of timing.

Halsey was the master of ceremonies for a luncheon at which Minnesota Governor Orville Freeman spoke and then immediately left to attend to official duties, which included tending to a liberal spending bill he was trying to pass through the legislature. Halsey moved back behind the lectern, waited until Freeman was on his way out the door of the ballroom, and hollered, "So long, Governor. Don't over-tax yourself."

The line went over so well that Halsey used it again years later on another Minnesota governor, Wendell Anderson.

As Halsey rose to speak on one occasion, a floral arrangement fell off the head table. Halsey watched the flowers tumble to the floor and, without missing a beat, quipped, "I don't understand that. I just took a Cloret."

Halsey's range, however, could span the gamut from funny to serious. While he had the ability to keep an audience in stitches with his humor, he proved to be able to elicit tears as well as laughs, and was often called upon to deliver eulogies.

"He could be touching without being maudlin," said

his daughter.

She added that, no matter what type of speaking her dad was called on to do, he kept notes of the material he delivered at each occasion. "He wanted to keep track of what stories he told to which groups and when, so that he wouldn't repeat them to the same people.

"The system worked well for him, although it was tricky when he spoke to inmate groups at the state prison in Stillwater. So many of the same people were back there year after year."

While Halsey took the time to make sure he was properly prepared for every speaking engagement, he could respond on short notice as well.

Sue Kennedy recalled a time when the regular speaker at her Morningside Woman's Club didn't show up. "Daddy happened to be there that day. Without any rehearsal, he and I went up front and put on a performance together.

"We could have made a great comedy duo."

Don Riley cited another occasion when, without any prior notice, Halsey was asked to say a few words. "He knew very little about the audience—in fact, he had to ask me what the banquet was all about. But within a couple of minutes, he had the people rolling in the aisles.

"That brain of his was always working overtime. He had a trigger mind and such a marvelous manner of injecting humor into all types of situations."

Halsey enjoyed speaking so much that the remuneration he received for his appearances was never of paramount importance to him.

"He was generous to a fault," said Sue. "For many years, he didn't take money for his speaking. I had to get on him to start charging a fee. Even then, he never asked for very much."

Paul Giel remembers a University of Minnesota Williams' Fund dinner that Halsey emceed in Giel's hometown of Winona, Minnesota. "To have Halsey as the master of ceremonies for the event was a particular thrill for me, as well as for the people down there," said Giel. "But he didn't want to take a fee.

"We drove down to Winona together and I told him, 'Halsey, that meeting hall is going to be packed tonight because of you. You're going to get a fee and it's going to be a good one compared to what you've been used to.'

"He finally took the money, but only after the other organizers and I had insisted on it."

Halsey continued his public appearances to the end.

In April of 1977, he was the grand marshal of the parade to commemorate the 90th anniversary of St. Louis Park, where Halsey had lived for more than half a century.

On December 14 of that year, little more than two weeks before his death, Halsey made his final speech. The site was The Little Wagon restaurant in downtown Minneapolis, and the occasion was a testimonial for Bob Sorenson, the restaurant's owner. Along with Halsey on the speaking program were a pair of his former newspaper colleagues, Dick Gordon and Bill Hengen.

Gordon recalls that Halsey received a standing ovation both as he was introduced and at the finish of his speech.

Halsey's greatest moment on stage, though, may have come in the early 1960s in Pasadena, California when he shared the rostrum with Bob Hope during a party prior to one of the Gophers' Rose Bowl appearances.

During Halsey's turn behind the mike, he wowed the audience to the point that, backstage, Hope—with a definite note of admiration in his voice—asked, "Who the hell is that guy?"

Halsey the Storyteller

For many Minnesota Twins fans in the 1960s, the best part of a baseball game was a rain delay. For it was on these occasions that Halsey Hall would fill time on the radio by regaling listeners with tales of past events and personalities associated with our national pastime.

Halsey's reputation as a raconteur spread throughout the American League and he soon found himself in demand from other team's broadcast crews as they sought ways to fill their air time during interruptions in the games. As a result of these appearances, he developed quite a following throughout the league.

The popularity he achieved with fans from other American League cities manifested itself in 1969, when the Twins were playing in New York on Halsey's birthday. Upon his arrival at Yankee Stadium that afternoon to prepare for the broadcast, Halsey found more than 400 birthday cards, sent by the New York fans, waiting for him. And, during the game that evening, birthday wishes were extended to him on the scoreboard, prompting an ovation from those in attendance.

It wasn't just during rain delays that Halsey excelled with the anecdotes. He could weave stories in between pitches while a game was in progress and, according to Bob Wolff, was a master at balancing the stories involving Minneapolis or St. Paul. "If he told three [Minneapolis] Millers stories, he'd even it out by telling three [St. Paul] Saints stories," said Wolff. "He knew so many stories that it was never a problem for him to do this."

It wasn't just the listeners of his broadcasts who

benefitted from his storytelling ability.

"He was a real blessing to have along on road trips," said Eddie Popowski, the Millers' manager in 1960. "We spent a lot of time traveling or sitting around hotel lobbies, waiting until it was time to go to the ball park. With all his stories, he really helped to pass the time. I could listen to him all day."

Bill Monbouquette, who pitched for the Millers in 1958, concurred and added, "He was the funniest man I ever met."

Wayne Courtney, the former mayor of Edina, Minnesota and the basketball coach at Roosevelt High School in Minneapolis from 1948 to 1968, was first exposed to Halsey and his stories many years before, when the pair officiated sports events together. "We once worked a game in Cambridge about 40 miles north of the Twin Cities. Halsey picked me up and, from the time I got in his car, he started telling baseball stories. He kept going with them nonstop all the way to Cambridge. After the game, we got back in the car to head home and he started telling the stories again.

"He told stories all the way up there and all the way back and the most amazing thing was that he never repeated a single one."

Calvin Griffith, the Twins' former owner, said that even if Halsey did repeat a story, it was still entertaining. "He'd never tell stories the same way, so, even if you had heard the story before, it was still new.

"When you sat around a table with Halsey and Dick Cullum, it was just like watching a comedy show. Dick was always Halsey's straight man. The two of them were quite a team when it came to telling stories. They could keep your tummy sore from laughing so much."

According to Norm McGrew, Halsey often gestured wildly in the course of telling a story. McGrew recalls

Halsey once creating a stir in an Orlando, Florida restaurant when he became particularly demonstrative. "It was during spring training following a Twins game on a Sunday afternoon," said McGrew. "Halsey was telling a story and started waving his arms around so much that the waiters thought he was having a seizure. They rushed over and asked if he needed a doctor."

"He was a master storyteller," said Ray Scott. "Halsey could keep people who had never before met him entertained for hours.

"We used to needle him about it. I'd say, 'Halsey, the only reason you can get away with all these stories is that you're too old for anyone else to disagree with what you say. You remember things that took place before the rest of us were born.' "

Indeed, much of the credit for Halsey's ability as a raconteur was given to his fantastic memory, which allowed him to recall incidents and anecdotes from years before.

Courtney remembers an occasion that illustrates Halsey's incredible recall. "My wife, Virginia, appeared in plays in the Morningside Theater Company with Halsey's daughter, Sue.

"Before one play, Sue introduced him to all 20 members in the cast. At the end of the performance, Halsey came backstage to congratulate them. As he did so, he greeted each member of the company by name after having met them only once."

"Halsey has a memory for faces, events, and people which creates envy," wrote *Minneapolis Star* columnist Bill Hengen in 1966. "There is nothing more mentally refreshing than to see someone approach him with the annoying, quizzing question, without offering a name, or 'I'll bet you don't remember me.'

And hear Halsey pinpoint a first—or last—name, and sometimes even the circumstance of the meeting."

"Halsey's memory going back in time was incredible," said Ray Christensen. "He might not remember what happened in the game the day before, but going back in history, he was infallible."

A promotional profile on Halsey written by the *Minneapolis Star-Journal* in 1944 read, "Halsey has an incredible memory; ask him who played in the 1927 Minnesota-Wisconsin game and how the score stood at the half, and he'll pop the answer right back at you..."

Despite the accolades he received in this department, Halsey was the first to admit that his memory was sometimes overrated. "I can remember some things, but not all," he once said.

Halsey's strength may have been not in recalling exact details, but in summoning remembrances of people, places, and events with which he had been associated.

Marshall Tanick, a Minneapolis attorney, relates an episode which illustrates what Halsey might or might not be expected to remember. "In the early days of the Twins," said Tanick, "Halsey hosted a post-game question-and-answer show on WCCO radio after each Sunday home game. In 1961 I participated on the program and stumped Halsey with a question concerning Mike Grady, a turn-of-the-century third baseman for the New York Giants, who committed four errors on one batted ball. For my efforts, I won an autographed Twins' baseball.

"Flash forward to 1968. I was in the midst of my tenure as the sports editor of the *Minnesota Daily* at the University of Minnesota when I appeared on the pre-game television show Halsey had at this time. The show consisted of a little chatter and a question for

Halsey. Figuring that I ought not break up a good thing, I again tried the Mike Grady question on Halsey—and once more stumped him.

"A few years later I ran into Halsey at a social event and introduced myself. He did not, of course, remember my name, but when I reminded him of my dual appearance with him, he immediately responded: 'You're the kid who fooled me twice about that third baseman who made four errors.'"

Whatever Halsey's secret as a storyteller may have been, it obviously worked. Even at the age of 78, he was still able to draw a crowd with his anecdotes.

Following a bridal dinner for his granddaughter, Kathy, in 1976, he stepped outside and soon found himself holding court on the front steps with some of the guests. Sue Kennedy says, "I still remember one of the guys, a college friend of Kathy's, running through the house hollering, 'Come on out. Halsey's telling stories.'"

Halsey's arsenal of stories covered a wide range of topics and sports, but most involved baseball. "You can sit around telling baseball stories and go five days without running out," he once said. "You couldn't do that with any other sport. There's something about baseball that lends itself to this."

No doubt some stories have followed Halsey to his grave, but many have been left behind to be enjoyed by future generations. What follows is a collection of stories told by Halsey over the years, in the words of the master himself.

One of Halsey's favorite stories involved Rosy Ryan, the Minneapolis Millers' general manager, and Lefty Gomez, the former Yankee pitcher whose antics had earned him the nickname "Goofy":

"It was during a mid-winter baseball banquet at the Nicollet Hotel that Ryan was presented with a set of golf clubs. Ryan and El Goof were staying at the Radisson, about six blocks away, and neither had brought an overcoat.

"It was about 15 below zero when Ryan, clubs over his shoulder, and Gomez set out for their hotel shortly after midnight. As they walked down Hennepin Avenue, a couple of other pedestrians gave Ryan a strange look.

"Gomez immediately went over to one and remarked, 'Do you know this crazy so-and-so wants me to go out and play 18 holes now?'"

Many of Halsey's former colleagues commented on how Halsey never spoke ill of anyone. A parable told often by Halsey sheds light on his philosophy in the people department:

"A man who was generally disliked departed this world. At his funeral, no one could think of anything good to say about him—until his barber stepped forward and said, 'He was easy to shave.'

"See, there's good in everyone."

Halsey's yarns could pop up anywhere. In a letter to University of Minnesota athletic director Marsh Ryman in 1971, Halsey threw in this story:

"As strange as things have been with the Twins this year, we have not had the spectacle that once nearly drove coach Vern Morgan to the nuthouse. Lissen: He is managing Fort Walton Beach in the then Class-D Florida State League. He has two Cubans who barely speak English; one is on first, the other on second with nobody out. Batter hits a long drive, looks uncatchable.

"The Cubans take off. The guy on second scores, the guy on first is at third and—the ball is caught. Now,

these guys do not know they have to retouch the bases going back, so what do they do? The guy on third CUTS ACROSS THE PITCHER'S MOUND TOWARD FIRST, THE GUY WHO SCORED CUTS ACROSS TO SECOND.

"The dumb bastards collide on the pitching mound, fall down—triple play!!"

Halsey told this one about the time he joined Bob Casey in the public-address booth at Met Stadium during a football game between the Vikings and New York Giants:

"There was a penalty on the Vikings for having an ineligible man downfield, but Bob missed the referee's signal and had to ask me what the penalty was for.

"I told him the Vikings had an illegitimate man down field and Casey repeats it just the way I told him: 'Vikings penalized 15 yards for an illegitimate man down field.'

"The crowd roared with laughter and we found out later that one of the Giants then yelled at the Vikings, 'Come on, you bastards, play ball.'"

While speaking at a banquet for the South Dakota Amateur Baseball Association, Halsey regaled the group with a description of the longest home run he had ever witnessed:

"It happened during a game in Lake Norden, South Dakota. The batter walloped a shot that landed in a gondola car passing by on the railroad tracks bordering the park. The home-run ball wasn't recovered until the train stopped in Watertown, 25 miles away!"

The shortest home run ever, claimed Halsey, was hit by Andy Oyler, a shortstop for the Minneapolis Millers from 1903 to 1909:

"It was in the late innings of a game played in a

steady drizzle at Nicollet Park. Oyler chopped at a low pitch and sent it straight down into the mud in front of home plate. Oyler circled the bases while the pitcher and catcher, and eventually the entire infield, tried to find the ball in the mud.

"Oyler completed his journey by sliding home in front of the tag of the second baseman, who had finally located the ball just five-and-a-half feet in front of home plate.

"That's a record which may last forever."

Halsey had these memories of a pair of Minnesota football greats. One, Pudge Heffelfinger, was a native of the state who went east and became a three-time All-American guard at Yale in the late 19th-century:

"Pudge was a giant who played forever, it seemed. He went back to Yale for a visit when he was 50 and worked out with the team. The Yale coach let Pudge put on a uniform and then said to his team, 'Be careful of this old man, for heaven's sake. He just wants to relive the old days.'

"A half-hour later, though, he called Pudge over and said, 'Would you please be careful? You're killing my players!'"

Another involved Earl Martineau, an All-American halfbalk for the Minnesota Gophers in the 1920s:

"Minnesota played Wisconsin in their 1922 homecoming game. The Badgers had a great back named Rollie Williams, who broke loose on one play. Only Martineau stood between Williams and the goal line, but two big blockers were roaring in to knock him out of Williams' path. Do you know what Earl did? He leaped over those two blockers, high in the air—like a fullback diving over the goal line for a touchdown—and nailed Williams before he could score.

"Greatest play I ever saw."

The majority of Halsey's stories, it seems, center on the colorful characters who had performed for the Minneapolis Millers and St. Paul Saints, the minor-league baseball teams that inhabited the Twin Cities prior to the arrival of the Minnesota Twins.

In July of 1977 Ken Ottoson, Larry Loeschen, and Frank Engdahl spent an evening with Halsey. The trio would name a former Miller or Saint, and Halsey would respond with a story about the player, to wit:

Ted Williams, who played with the Millers in 1938 and won the American Association Triple Crown before graduating to the majors and a Hall-of-Fame career with the Boston Red Sox:

"Ted Williams playing at Nicollet Park! Wouldn't you think he'd hit 80 home runs? He did hit 43 and also led the league in batting average, RBI's, runs scored, total bases, and walks. Not a bad year for a 20-year-old kid.

"But Ted was temperamental. [Millers' manager] Donie Bush once went to owner Mike Kelley and said, 'Either that kid goes or I go.' Kelley replied, 'We're going to miss you, Donie.'

"That was the end of that!"

Roy Campanella, who broke the color barrier when he appeared behind the plate for the St. Paul Saints (a Brooklyn Dodger farm club) in 1948:

"When Campy joined the Dodgers in 1948, [Dodger president] Branch Rickey told him, "You're the best catcher we have, but I'd like you to go to St. Paul. Our club there needs help. For the Saints, he hit 13 home runs and had 39 RBIs after 39 games. Then Bruce Edwards, the Dodgers' catcher, got hurt and Campy got called up. The rest is history.

"He always looked overweight. But, you know, you

have to be in shape if you catch 300 games in a year, including four in one day, which he did in his days in the Negro Leagues.

"He was a great catcher and a tremendous hitter. You could see even then that he would wind up in the Hall of Fame."

Another Negro League veteran, Dave Barnhill, who finally got his chance in organized baseball with the Minneapolis Millers in 1949. Barnhill and Ray Dandridge were the first blacks to play for the Millers:

"I'll never forget the time Barnhill struck out 16 Saints in one game at Lexington Park. The Saints were convinced he was scuffing the ball and they kept squawking at the umpire, 'Look at the ball!' But the umpire could never find anything wrong with the ball.

"The secret was that Ray Dandridge, the third baseman, would nick the ball on his belt buckle. As you know, the ball is thrown around the infield between outs. Ray would get it and give it the treatment.

"Not only was Barnhill a switch-hitter, he was also ambidextrous in throwing. He didn't do it with the Millers, but he threw both ways when he pitched in the Negro Leagues."

Ray Dandridge:

"He always threw a man out by a step-and-a-half. I don't care if the man was fast or was so slow that he looked like he was pushing a safe to first base—Dandy would manage to throw him out by a step-and-a-half. It was uncanny.

"We Minneapolis writers had been raving about Dandridge when somebody hit a ground ball to him. Dandy just lobbed it over to first and one of the St. Paul writers said, 'Ha! Is that the great Dandridge?'

"'Wait a minute,' I told him. Sure enough, here comes

*a perfect bunt to Dandridge and, zip, the guys's out
by—you guessed it—a step-and-a-half.*

*"He was a great ballplayer—a good hitter, good
fielder, and good runner. He ran like a crab with those
bowlegs, but, oh, could he scamper!"*

Willie Mays, who performed so spectacularly for the
Millers in the spring of 1951 that he was called up to the
New York Giants after only 35 games:

*"Do you remember how, when Ted Williams took
batting practice, the other club would stop and watch?
Well, they used to stop and watch Willie when he was
taking outfield practice. That's how good he was in the
field.*

*"Willie might have broken every record in the history
of the American Association. In late May, though, we
were playing an exhibition game in Sioux City when
Leo Durocher, the Giants' manager, called and said
they needed him in New York.*

*"'But Mr. Leo, I like it here and I'd like to stay,' said
Willie. Durocher said, 'Willie, what are you hitting?'
When Willie told him his batting average was .477 at
that time, there was about a 15-second pause followed
by Leo screaming into the phone, 'You get your ass on
the next plane to New York!'"*

Bruno Haas, an outfielder for the Saints from 1920
to 1930, who also played briefly in the National Football League.

*"Bruno was the author of the diving catch. He should
have worn a glove on his naval. He was always diving
at fly balls; I sometimes think he would purposely slow
up on a ball just so he could dive for it!"*

Clyde "Pea Ridge" Day, a hard-drinking man who
pitched for the Millers in the early 1930s before killing
himself by slitting his throat with a hunting knife:

"Clyde 'Pea Ridge' Day came from Pea Ridge, Arkansas. I don't know his measurements, but he was a big, husky, barrel-chested guy, and he took a big windup. He'd come around twice in a circle, and, as he was doing it, he'd emit the loudest hog yell you ever heard. (He was once the champion hog caller of Arkansas.)

"Once, when he was pitching for the Kansas City Blues, the entire Kansas City team was compelled to leave a fashionable Milwaukee hotel because Pea Ridge went to the central part of the lobby, while an orchestra was playing, and emitted his piercing yell!

"I once asked him, 'How in the world do you get to Pea Ridge?'

"'Well,' he replied, 'you take the Rio Grande Railroad and you get off at the Mill Creek station and you walk through the woods, grab a hanging tree branch, and swing on it. When you land, you're in Pea Ridge!'"

Fabian Gaffke, a strong right-handed hitter for the Millers in the 1930s:

"Only once did I ever see what happened to Fabian Gaffke one hot afternoon at Lexington Park.

"The Saints were hosting the Millers. The St. Paul player-manager, Red Kress, was playing first base and Dwain Sloat was pitching. Tom Sheehan was coaching at third for the Millers and Gaffke was at bat when Sloat wound up and floated a half-speed pitch to the plate.

"Suddenly, the ball either burst in half or somehow became a double baseball. "Gaffke fell back, almost screaming. Sheehan went to his knees, and slowly started toward Sloat with clasped hands, pleading for mercy. Sloat laughed.

"What had happened? Some player had thrown Sloat a ball which had been knocked foul, but Dwain had already received a new one from the umpire. He had

shown the two to Kress and asked, 'What shall I do?'
and Red answered, 'Throw 'em both!'"

Buzz Arlett, a powerful switch-hitter who didn't join
the Millers until five weeks into the season in 1934, but
still managed to win the American Association home-
run crown:

"One of the finest baserunners ever seen at Nicollet
Park was—don't laugh now—Buzz Arlett. The beloved
big guy was a good baserunner for two reasons: daring
and instinct. Furthermore, when you, as a baseman, see
a six-foot-five, 225-pound man bearing down on you, it
is easy to think of home and mother and go ahead, pal,
the baseline is yours.

"There was the time Arlett set out for a two-base hit.
He slid into second. Out! But the shortstop dropped the
ball. Buzz then decided to steal third. He was out there,
too, but another dropped throw saved him. Then came
a wild pitch. The pitcher covered the plate as Buzz
barreled home. The throw was there about ten feet
ahead of Arlett, but the pitcher couldn't handle it.

"Buzz had been out at three bases and yet he still
scored. Top that one, ladies and gentlemen."

Babe Barna, the oft-booed darling of Nicollet Park
who twice led the American Association in home runs
while playing for the Millers in the 1940s:

"Babe was a great big gentle giant who would walk
through fire if the boss asked him. But the big guy had
a sort of nonchalant way of doing things at times, and,
because of that, some fans got on him.

"You know how fans love to pick on great big guys
who look like bullies, and I know that Babe was the
policeman for the club. One day he walked over to the
opposing dugout at Nicollet and challenged anyone to
come out...even by two's or three's, but he didn't get any
takers."

Jack Cassini, a speedy leadoff man for the Saints, who also played for the Memphis Chicks in the Southern Association after leaving St. Paul:

"Jack Cassini played one of the greatest tricks in the history of baseball when he was with Memphis. The pitcher for the other team was one of those guys with a terrific windup, much like Luis Tiant later on. He would bend w-a-a-y back. And, of course, every pitcher sighting a hitter gets a bead. It might be the visor of his cap or the batter's shoulder.

"Well, Cassini's at bat with the winning run on third. He's a right-handed hitter and, as the pitcher goes into his wild windup, Cassini turns around. Now, he stays in the right-handed batter's box, but his rump is toward home plate.

"The pitcher lets fly, it's a wild pitch by three feet, and Memphis wins the game.

"Only Cassini could think of something like that."

Ray "Old Blue" Moore, who pitched for the Saints from 1952 to 1954 and returned to the state in 1961 as a relief pitcher for the Twins:

"Ray Moore had a hunting dog that he called Old Blue, so Ray also became known as Old Blue. A great starting pitcher for the Saints and a great reliever for the Twins, he used to brag about his dog. He said it was the only dog he knew that could swim on its back... which I still want to see.

"Ray was a great hunter and fisherman. One day he set out with the dog, who thinks they're going hunting. But instead of picking up a rifle, Ray grabs his fishing pole. And the dog? He starts digging up worms.

"Well, at least that's the story."

Tom Sheehan, a great pitcher for the St. Paul Saints who later managed the Millers. Sheehan won 31 games for the Saints in 1923:

"Tom was one of the great storytellers of all time. He pitched for Hollywood in the Pacific Coast League in the 1930s and told me of the time he faced Mike Hunt, a redoubtable slugger, with two out in the ninth.

"There were no lights at this park and it was getting very dark. Tom threw a strike. As he finished his delivery, he didn't retreat to the mound but, rather, held his position. Another pitch; another strike. And Tom stayed right where his delivery had left him. His next pitch was strike three and the game was over.

"As they walked off the field, Hunt said to Sheehan, 'Boy, you sure had something on that last pitch.'

"Sheehan replies, 'I sure did. And if I'd have thrown another one, I'd have hit you right on the chin with my fist!'"

Dave Altizer, probably the greatest shortstop in the history of the Millers, who played for the team from 1910 to 1918:

"Dave was a great base runner, but once he tried to steal third when the bases were loaded.

"Pongo Joe Cantillon, the manager, said to him, 'I don't blame you, Dave. You had a hell of a lead!'"

Another Millers' story, involving owner Mike Kelley, was told by Halsey to Patrick Reusse of the *St. Paul Pioneer Press* in 1974:

"Kelley had a reputation of being cheap, but he always insisted on first-class hotels. In 1946, though, when Zeke Bonura was manager, Kelley got talked into having spring training in Bay St. Louis, Mississippi, Zeke's hometown.

"The place was a burgh. The first day we have a game, Zeke asks Kelley if he can get the brothers and sisters from the Catholic school he went to and a few

other friends in free. There must have been 4,000 people in the stands—all free. And we didn't draw five people the rest of the spring.

"Then we were barnstorming north and Kelley split the squad for a game in Selma, Alabama. He's in the hotel and hears these sounds—like bugs flying and crawling and rats running—and goes down to complain.

"The clerk says, 'Sir, I'll have you know that Jefferson Davis slept in that room.'

"Mike replies, 'Well, the son of a bitch must still be rattling around up there.'"

On the subject of chewing tobacco:

"Recently a woman complained about the close-up camera shots of Sparky Lyle, the Yankee pitcher, and his monumental chew of tobacco.

"Shucks, Ma'am, 'twarn't nuthin. Biggest chew anyone ever saw belonged to Nellie Fox, the White Sox second baseman. Now, Nellie was only five-foot-seven and that wad of his made his face completely lopsided, making it, really, only half a face.

"Oldtimers were the real champs, though. Tough, too. Rosy Ryan once told about an old Giant catcher, Frank Bowerman, who fell rounding first, breaking a leg. He calmly reached down, rubbed tobacco juice on the protruding bone, and ran on to second."

Halsey's one-liners were often as memorable as his longer stories. On rickety Nicollet Park, the home of the Minneapolis Millers from 1896 to 1955:

"The place was so run down that every time a foul ball hit the roof, all the toilets would flush."

On a towering pop up by Twins' slugger Harmon Killebrew:
"That would have been a home run in an elevator."

One of Halsey's final stories appeared in the column he wrote for the *Twin Cities Free Press* up to the time of his death:
"There was the time a would-be flowery writer covered a holocaust in a mining community in Pennsylvania. He started out, 'God sits tonight on the hills of Cokeburg.' The Morse operator, who was ticking off the story, yelled, 'Just a moment, kid. I got a message from your boss.' And the message:

"'DROP EVERYTHING AND INTERVIEW GOD. GET PICTURES.'"

Halsey was a pioneer of the "Zebra stripes" for referees.

Halsey the Referee

Although Halsey Hall was widely known as a media personality, many fans and participants in sports in the Upper Midwest first knew him as one of the area's premier referees. Halsey officiated football in the days before facemasks, and basketball at a time when there was still a center jump after every basket.

Babe LeVoir, a University of Minnesota great under Bernie Bierman and later Halsey's broadcast partner for Gopher games, was one who first became acquainted with him in Halsey's role as a referee. Halsey officiated many of the football games in which LeVoir played for Marshall High School in Minneapolis in the late 1920s and early 1930s.

Likewise, Jules Perlt—who became the public-address announcer for Minnesota football and basketball and served as the "Voice of the Gophers" for more than half a century—was first exposed to Halsey as a referee, while Perlt played basketball at St. Paul Humboldt High School. "Halsey was just starting as an official around the time I was graduating in 1921," said Perlt. "Off the court, he was a happy-go-lucky guy, but he took his officiating seriously and was considered a very good referee."

For more than 20 years, officiating provided Halsey not only with another means of supplementing his income, but yet another way of being involved with games he loved. It also made an already overloaded schedule and lifestyle even more frenetic.

It wasn't unusual for Halsey to officiate more than one game in a day; at times, he even did double duty by combining his roles as a referee and newspaper reporter. For example, on Friday, September 27, 1929,

Halsey officiated a Minneapolis City Conference high-school football game between Edison and West in the afternoon and a college gridiron contest between Gustavus Adolphus and Stout in the evening. He then banged out a story on the Gustavus-Stout game that appeared the next day in the *Minneapolis Journal.*

Interestingly, Halsey never umpired baseball, his favorite sport; his officiating activities were confined to basketball and football, primarily at the amateur level. He did, however, have the chance to work games at the major-league level during the first two occasions that Minneapolis was represented by a team in the National Football League.

From 1921 through 1924, the Minneapolis Marines played in the NFL. Later in the decade, the Minneapolis Redjackets were members of the National Football League for two years. Both the Marines and Redjackets played their home games at Nicollet Park. Halsey twice served as a referee and five times as a head linesman in games involving the Minneapolis teams. The pay scale for NFL officials in those days, Halsey recalled, was $35 a game for a referee and $25 a game for a head linesman or other official.

Along with one of his early partners in the trade, Johnny Getchell, Halsey has been credited with introducing this area to what is now a standard article of attire for referees—the black-and-white striped shirt.

"Halsey and Getchell were the first referees I ever saw with the 'zebra stripes,'" said Angelo Giuliani, who became acquainted with the pair while he was playing basketball at St. Thomas Military Academy in St. Paul in 1928.

Halsey also referred to the shirts in a 1970 letter to University of Minnesota athletic director Marsh Ryman. "Did you know I virtually pioneered the striped referee shirt?" he wrote. "To my knowledge, when I began wearing it to work basketball games, it was the first time such a shirt had been seen in Minneapolis."

Sports author and historian Stan Carlson said Halsey was noted as a rules expert. "He studied the rule books for all sports," said Carlson. "Not only was this important for him as a referee, but it sometimes gave him material for his newspaper column. Now and then, he would describe a trick play and then explain the rule interpretation that applied."

Halsey's success as a referee (or as a "robber," as he referred to the profession) was not simply because of his knowledge of the rules, however. John Sammon, who was to become a well-known official himself, said he learned a lesson from Halsey while playing basketball at Minneapolis De La Salle High School.

"Halsey had a delicate way of handling irate players and coaches," said Sammon. "He kept control of the game without being overbearing."

As an example, Sammon cited a game De La Salle played against a highly-rated parochial-school team from Chicago, St. Mel's, in 1929. "Halsey refereed all of our home games that year. We never had any trouble with the officials, mainly because we always won.

"Against St. Mel's, though, we fell behind and began complaining about some of the calls. When I started arguing with Halsey, he very gently stopped the game and said, 'Now, Johnny, I've refereed 50 percent of your games this year and you won every one. I'm the same referee tonight that I was during those games. You just keep playing and don't pay any attention to the referees.'

"He was a high-class guy, and I later tried to pattern my officiating style after his."

Rollie Johnson and Halsey, broadcast partners for

Gopher football, also officiated together for many years. Johnson recalled that, even though Halsey took his duties seriously, his sense of humor still came through during the games. "We enjoyed refereeing together," said Johnson. "His funloving nature popped up all the time.

"We'd be working a football game together and, after spotting the ball, Halsey would walk past me and mutter something funny under his breath. I'd start to laugh and, pretty soon, all the coaches in Minneapolis and St. Paul started wondering about us.

"They'd be saying, 'What's with that Hall and Johnson? Every time you see them, they're whispering to each other and laughing.' Halsey could get away with it, though, because he was an outstanding official."

Willie Kolesar, the last in a line of brothers to star in football and basketball at Minneapolis Roosevelt High School, remembers an incident involving Halsey as a referee in a game at West High in October of 1932. After returning a punt 80 yards for a touchdown, Kolesar lined up to kick the point after.

"Just before the ball was snapped, Halsey said to me, 'I've got a nickel that says you won't make it.' Well, I split the uprights with that kick and Mr. Hall pushed a buffalo-head nickel down into my high-top shoes.

"I was happy to get it. Nickels were hard to come by in those days."

As a referee on another occasion, Halsey became an unwilling focal point in a key game for the state Catholic high-school championship between Cretin and St. Thomas Academy. Cretin scored the game's only touchdown, aided by Halsey, who accidentally collided with the last St. Thomas defender and took him out of the play. "Cretin wanted to award me a letter for my efforts on their behalf in the game," Halsey recalled later with a laugh.

While Halsey could always see the lighter side in any situation, the same was true of his colleagues. Frank Cleve summarized his former partner's career as an official at a testimonial dinner for Halsey in 1966. "I was going to send Halsey a Christmas card one year," said Cleve, "but I couldn't find any in Braille."

Halsey's One and Only

Happy Anniversary, Sula Dear

Down the halls of mem'ry and the corridors of time
Stroll so many happenings that lend themselves to rhyme;
Touch of fingers in a dance that brought us face to face,
Then it was that clouds did part and things fell into place.

Lights grew low amidst the glow, the music stopped and then
Joy arose within my heart as seldom comes to men;
It was fifty years or more as mortals measure time,
Yet no form of measuring can chart our love sublime.

12/20/74

At the same time a young sailor named Halsey Hall was carrying out his service commitment in Duluth, Minnesota, a schoolteacher named Marguerite Sula Bornman was also residing in the city.

The daughter of German immigrants, Sula Bornman was born, with a twin brother who died at birth, on April 24, 1897 in Emmaus, Pennsylvania. Sula's father, a barber, died when she was four. Following the death of her mother nine years later, Sula moved to Fargo, North Dakota to live with her sister, Katie Marcks, who was 14 years her senior, and Katie's husband, Stanley.

After graduating from Fargo High School in 1915, Sula crossed the Red River of the North into Minnesota and enrolled at Moorhead Normal School (a training facility for teachers that eventually became Moorhead State University). Upon completion of the two-year program, she returned to North Dakota to begin teaching school in Dickinson.

Sula came to Duluth to teach at Fairmount School in 1918 and moved in with the MacIver Family at 1212 E. 2nd Street. One Saturday night during her first year in the city, she and a gentleman friend attended a dance at the Shrine Temple.

During the course of the evening, she noticed a sailor poking fun at her by pretending to stroke some non-existent whiskers on his face, an allusion to the age of her older date. By chance, during a Circle Two-Step number a few minutes later, the circle stopped with she and the sailor standing opposite one another, thus bringing about the first meeting between Sula Bornman and Halsey Hall.

While exactly what transpired the rest of the evening is unclear, soon after Halsey began courting her. Sula, however, maintained a blasè attitude about the relationship.

Dorothy MacIver Pearson, who was ten years old at the time that Sula boarded with her family, recalled Halsey arriving for a date and waiting on the front porch while Sula got ready. "My mother told Sula to have the young man come in, but Sula said 'He can wait on the porch. He's just a sailor.'"

Halsey wasn't the only man in Sula's life while she lived in Duluth. The following year, after moving into an apartment two blocks from the MacIver home, she became friendly with Frank Duffy, the school system's penmanship supervisor. "I remember Frank carrying bags of groceries to Sula's apartment, and she'd cook dinner for him," said Dorothy Pearson.

Actually, Sula had no shortage of suitors during this period. Sue Kennedy says that, at one time or another, her mother was engaged to three different men, although only one of the relationships ended in matrimony.

This occurred after Sula moved to Minneapolis for the 1922 school year and renewed ties with her former sailor friend who, by this time, was once again a civilian, and working as a sportswriter for the *St. Paul Pioneer Press.* Apparently, Sula no longer required Halsey to wait on the porch; soon after, the two became engaged.

The wedding was set for December 22, 1922 in London, Wisconsin where Sula's older brother, Charles, was a minister in a Moravian parish. For Sula, the date coincided with the Christmas holiday from her teaching duties. For Halsey, the date was even more convenient as it corresponded with a trip to cover the opening of the United States Amateur Hockey League season in Milwaukee.

Charles presided over the nuptials while his wife, Millie, played the piano. The Bornman's neighbors, Leo and Elsie Blaschka, served as witnesses.

Fifty years later, on the occasion of their Silver anniversary, Sula recalled the event. "I had made my own dress in Millie's sewing room—black floor length with silver lace and rose-flowered belt and sash and black brocaded slippers. Halsey wanted me to keep the dress forever, but I won out and eventually used it to make living room pillows and a davenport cover.

"I wanted to be married in the country church, but the church was in one county and the parsonage in another, so we had to be married in the house. Millie collected house plants from the neighbors and made a beautiful alter in the bay window. Halsey wore a pin-striped suit and I had an armful of pale pink roses as Charles read the words about 7 o'clock."

With Sula still in her wedding dress and Halsey clad in a raccoon coat, the newlyweds boarded a train for Milwaukee, where they spent their wedding night at the Martin Hotel.

The following evening, they saw the St. Paul Athletic Club team drop its season opener to the Milwaukee Brewers. Before the game, Moose Goheen, St. Paul's high-scoring defenseman (and one of Halsey's favorite players), couldn't resist a dig at the new groom.

"Who's that lovely flower with you?" he asked Halsey and then feigned incredulity when told it was his bride.

The couple returned to the Twin Cities and moved into their new home at 3149 Ramona (which later was given the new address of 3231 Alabama Avenue) in suburban St. Louis Park. Sula had told Halsey she was more interested in having a house than a wedding ring.

She eventually got the ring, too (on her 15th anniversary), but, according to Sue, this attitude was typical of her mother. "She was an enormously practical woman, completely unlike Daddy.

"They were opposites in many ways. For example, she had a real temper and Daddy didn't fight, so they got along fine."

Another example of their differences was Halsey's love of center stage and Sula's willingness to stay in the shadows. "At the parties they hosted," recalled Sue, "Mother would stay in the kitchen doing the cooking while Daddy held court."

Part of Sula's reason for staying in the background was a self-consciousness over what she perceived as a accent as a result of her Pennsylvania Dutch upbringing that made it difficult to enunciate words beginning with v or w. "She had no accent," maintains Sue, "but she was sure she would say something like, 'It's a wery vonderful day.' She'd actually leave the room if she was asked to speak at a party, although she did love to participate in games like charades that didn't require talking."

Regardless of the reasons, however, it appears that Sula just never shared her husband's desire to be the center of attention. "When my best friend, Ruth Hirshfield, got married," Sue recalled, "Mother made the bridesmaid hats but let Daddy deliver them. This way he could be the big shot.

"It was like this with her garden, too. She would let Daddy hoe the rows of corn so he could say he grew it, although she was the one who had done all the work."

It never bothered Sula to see Halsey receive credit for her efforts, even with her garden of which she was especially proud. Sue says her mother managed to maintain a beautiful row of flowers alongside the house in spite of Halsey. "Every day when he'd leave for work, he'd back out right over her peonies. But somehow they always survived."

The fact that Sula was content to avoid the spotlight in which her husband basked, however, did not mean that she was not her own person. "She was the original woman's libber," said Sue. "Even though married teachers were frowned upon at that time, she kept teaching after the wedding right up until she became pregnant with me in 1926.

"She wanted to be known as Sula Hall, not Mrs. Halsey Hall, and she was even able to get a charge card in her own name. This was long before these things became fashionable.

"On another occasion she sold some furniture to an antique dealer. When the payment check arrived, it was made out to Halsey Hall. She sent it back and insisted that they issue a new check payable to Sula Hall."

Sula's independence and practicality were evident in her attitudes toward dating and marriage, her daughter recalled. "Mother also said a woman should bring mad money on a date in case she had to take a cab home, and, that when she got married, she should have her own checking account so she'd have enough money in case she ever got divorced.

"She'd also tell me that if she died before Daddy, that I was to come over and get all the silver and her jewelry. She was convinced some woman would glom onto Daddy, and that it would all be gone within six weeks."

For the most part, Sula was a direct woman, but one thing she did try to cover up was the difference in age between she and Halsey. She was 13 months older than her husband, but she told her daughter that the difference was only one month, maintaining that she had been born in 1898. She was tripped up, however, in a strange manner, according to Sue. "One day she showed me a picture of the gravestone of her twin brother who had died at birth. The inscription on the marker read 'Baby Boy Bornman—Born April 24, 1897.'

"So it was a from a gravestone of all things that I learned my mother's real age."

Sula may have had her idiosyncracies, but in describing her mother, Sue emphasizes her giving nature. "In 1932 Gram [Corinne Hall, Halsey's stepgrandmother] came to live with us. She was an invalid by this time, confined to a wheelchair, and for six years Mother took care of her. When it became too much for mother to handle, Gram finally moved into a vocational home and spent the final months of her life there.

"Right after that happened, her sister's husband lost his job. Once again, Mother opened up her house and Katie and Stanley came to live with us until he could get back on his feet."

In addition to a generous nature, Sula shared another trait with Halsey—an aversion to air travel.

Sue said the only flights her mother ever took were to Los Angeles and back for the 1965 World Series between the Twins and Dodgers. "Mother was allowed to fly free on the Twins' charter and she said, 'If Calvin [Griffith, Twins' owner] is going to pay, then I'm going to fly.'"

For the most part, though, Sula and Halsey had few similarities. The differences they possessed, however, were the type that seemed to complement one another. "She may have let Daddy do the talking," said Sue, "but she was the real force."

Sue, Halsey, and Sula take a break from the rigors of Spring Training at Daytona Beach in 1939.

Halsey the Family Man

"Mother always said it took her four years to get pregnant and another five to recover," said Sue Hall Kennedy. "I don't think the whole process was any easier on Daddy.

"Maybe that's the reason I'm an only child."

Suzanne Eugenia Hall was born on Wednesday, May 18, 1927 at Fairview Hospital in south Minneapolis.

While she doesn't have any firsthand recall of the event, Sue says she later learned plenty about the details of her birth from her mother. "I was told that when it was time for Mother to enter the hospital to have me, she didn't want to go," said Sue. "She thought she could just go out to the garage and have the baby by herself!

"To convince her that this wasn't the proper place to have a child, Daddy got her in the car and had to drive her around Lake Calhoun at least three times before he persuaded her that she really had to get to the hospital.

"When they arrived at the hospital, she was assigned a room, but my father wasn't allowed to join her. Daddy knew she didn't want to be left alone, so he went outside, sneaked up the fire escape, crawled through a window into the room, and jumped into bed with her.

"When it was time for me to be born, they stood him out of the way in a corner of the delivery room. From there, he observed my entry into the world."

Sue also knows that her birth occurred in the morning because, soon after the blessed event, Halsey rushed off to Nicollet Park to cover that afternoon's game between the Millers and Milwaukee Brewers.

Contrary to what one might guess, the proud father did not distribute cigars to his press-box colleagues, nor did he make any type of announcement about his new daughter. In fact, it wasn't until the following day that Halsey let anyone in on the news that he was a father.

"Daddy didn't want anyone to know I had been born until he had a better chance to look at me," said Sue. "As for Mother, she couldn't figure out why she wasn't getting any visitors."

Even though she was an only child, Sue was hardly alone as she grew up. "I always resented the term 'spoiled only child,'" said Sue. "That was never the case with me. It seemed like there was always someone living with us who needed attention. When I was five, Gram [Halsey's step-grandmother] moved in with us. She was an invalid—in a wheelchair—and Mother cared for her.

"Gram stayed with us for six years and then my mother's sister and her husband moved in for another three years."

Away from home, Sue still found herself surrounded by people. In 1937, she began joining her father for a portion of the Minneapolis Millers spring-training regimen, first in Daytona Beach, Florida, and later in New Braunfels, Texas. She reports that the players were always willing to assist her with her homework. "Not everyone could say she had Andy Cohen [the Millers' star second baseman] as an algebra tutor," recalls Sue.

But even with all these adults keeping her company as she grew up, Sue reports that, in many ways, Halsey always tried to be the "one and only" in her life.

"When I was a kid, he wouldn't let anyone else play Santa Claus for me. He had to be the one. And while I had a godmother—my Aunt Katie—I never had a godfather.

"We never even had any pets to speak of. We did have a cat once for all of three days. He spent the whole time under the couch before he finally ran away."

But Halsey couldn't be his daughter's "one and only" forever, and, on February 18, 1949, the Hall clan grew a notch when Sue married Bill Kennedy. "Picking the date for the wedding got to be a real chore," says Sue. "Originally, we planned on getting married in June of that year, right after I graduated from college at the University of Minnesota. A couple of my girlfriends were already planning weddings for that month, though, so we decided to move ours up to the spring.

"March was out because Daddy would be gone to spring training with the Millers. We finally decided on February 18th and, wouldn't you know it, the weather was almost spring-like that day. It hit 44 degrees."

The nuptials took place at the Hennepin Avenue United Methodist Church in south Minneapolis with the reception at the family home. Bill and Sue didn't remain long at the reception, however. They changed clothes at a neighbor's house and headed back downtown to the Nicollet Hotel, where they spent their wedding night. The next day the newlyweds were Chicago bound for their honeymoon, with train tickets given to them by Halsey and Sula.

Even though the Halls had lost a daughter, the family remained close—both emotionally and geographically. After the birth of their first child in 1951, Bill and Sue moved into a home at 3224 Zarthan Avenue in St. Louis Park, almost directly behind Halsey and Sula's house.

"We were the closest-knit family of any I knew," said Sue. "A lot of our friends kidded us about moving into a house right next to my parents, but it was a good arrangement.

"Even though we were so close, they never came over without being invited. And Mother insisted that Daddy leave us alone on Bill's day off. They were careful not to impose.

"We did spend a lot of time together, though. We'd play bridge and have dinner with them nearly every Sunday night, but it was always with the understanding that, if plans with other people came up, it was okay to cancel.

"I'd also see them almost every morning after Bill left for work. From our porch, I could see Mother in the garden with her flowers. I'd signal to her and she and Daddy would come over for coffee.

"We spent a lot of time together. We were best friends."

Bill and Sue Kennedy also produced three grandchildren for Halsey and Sula: William Halsey, born May 23, 1951; Kathryn Sula, born March 24, 1953; and Cynthia Eugenia, born March 21, 1956.

According to Sue, her father—who was an only child and was to be the father of only one child himself—had to learn firsthand that it was possible to love more than one child. "When he found out I was pregnant for the second time, he was amazed. He couldn't understand how I'd be able to love more than one at a time.

"He found out for himself, though, that it was possible. I'd never seen a more devoted and doting grandfather than him."

The fact that Billy, his first grandchild, was born on his birthday became a source of pride to Halsey. "Of course," said Sue, "he did kid around and fuss about how no one would remember his birthday anymore.

"He got even more excited when Billy started showing signs of being left-handed because, as he explained to me, left-handed pitchers made more money." (Sue

Sula and Halsey in 1935.

Halsey became a father-in-law on February 18, 1949 when his daughter Sue married Bill Kennedy.

Two years later he became a grandfather. From left to right: Cindy, Kathy, and Billy.

Halsey watches Kathy on the trampoline at Queen Anne Kiddieland, a small amusement park in Bloomington, Minnesota.

Halsey, Sula, and grandson Bill in 1972.

Halsey with granddaughter Cindy in 1959.

Bill and Sue sometimes joined Halsey on Twins' road trips. This one, to Washington, included a visit with President Lyndon Johnson.

Halsey's Hall of Fame: his family.
Back row—Son-in-law Bill and daughter Sue Kennedy.
Front row—Grandson Bill with his wife Shari and son Adam; granddaughters Cindy and Kathy.

added that it wasn't unusual for her dad to reach such conclusions or to make such seemingly divergent connections. "Our family doctor was Bill Proffitt, who later became the team physician for the Twins. Daddy picked him to be our doctor because, as he said, 'As a football player in college he had good hands, so he must be a good doctor.'")

When Kathy and Cindy got older, Sue says her dad enjoyed going to lunch with one or both of them, but not letting on to anyone that they were related. "That way, people would think he was going out with some young gal. He liked making people wonder like that."

For Halsey, being a grandfather meant an opportunity to revert to some of the pleasures of his youth. A fan of amusement parks ever since he accompanied his father to the magnificent Wonderland park on Lake Street, Halsey frequently took his grandkids to such fun spots as Excelsior Amusement Park on the shores of Lake Minnetonka and Queen Anne Kiddieland on the beltline in Bloomington, as well as to the Midway at the State Fair.

Halsey was particularly fond of springing surprises on his family. "He loved surprises—when they were his idea," Sue said. "If he was going to take Mother and me along to spring training, he often wouldn't tell us until the night before we were to leave.

"He wasn't practical. He didn't realize all the preparations Mother had to make before she could leave—arranging to have her plants watered, the mail taken in—but we always managed."

Bill and Sue joined Halsey on a road trip with the Twins for the first time in 1962 and, once again, the news came as a surprise to them. "Daddy called from Kansas City and told us if we could get there by the next day that we could fly with him and the team to Los Angeles.

"This was his surprise. He knew all along he would be doing this, but I guess he figured it would be no fun telling us weeks ahead."

Bill and Sue got Sula to look after the children, took the train to Kansas City, and joined the team on the charter flight to the West Coast. For Sue, the journey marked her first trip on an airplane. "Even though I had been married for 13 years and had three children by then," she said, "it was important to Daddy that he be with me when I was doing things like making my first airplane trip."

Another surprise awaited Bill and Sue a few years later even though, on this occasion, Halsey had informed them well in advance that they were welcome to join him on a road trip to Washington. What they didn't know was that Hubert Humphrey, then the vice president of the United States, had arranged a tour of the White House for the Twins, as well as a meeting with President Lyndon Johnson.

"We found out about all this the night before we left," said Sue. "Dad asked Bill if he was bringing along a white shirt. When Bill asked why, Daddy said, 'Because you're going to be meeting the President of the United States.'

"That's the way he liked breaking news—never in a direct way, but by asking something like 'Are you taking along a white shirt?' It certainly was an exciting trip for us, though, and it was especially fun to meet President Johnson."

Most of the road trips Halsey took, out of necessity, were without his family. But Halsey was a faithful letter writer, and every day Sula and Sue could count on a letter from him. He would send the original to one and the carbon copy to the other (always taking great care to alternate between who got the original and who got the copy).

His letters, which were written on hotel stationery or Twins letterhead (or anything else that was convenient at the time), never contained an exact date, but merely the day of the week, time, and a one-word weather report, e. g. Sat. noon, nice.

The salutation often contained a reference to "My Sues" (which he apparently felt was enough to cover both Sue and Sula), and, without fail, the letters concluded with a poem that he concocted on the spot.

In 1958, Bill and Sue moved from their home in St. Louis Park to a house on Sunnyside Avenue in Morningside (which later was annexed and became part of the city of Edina) approximately three miles away. Even though they were no longer virtual next-door neighbors, the closeness between the Kennedys and the Halls remained.

The Sunday night dinners together endured, and Halsey and Sula, until their final days, continued to dote upon their grandchildren.

A great deal of Halsey lives on with his daughter, who inherited many of his traits and knacks and found a way to put them to good use following his death. On May 18, 1979—her 52nd birthday—Sue appeared before a local civic organization and talked about her memories of her father.

So much public interest remained in her father that Sue found herself in demand as a speaker before audiences throughout the Twin Cities.

Until she and her husband moved to Tampa, Florida in 1982, Sue appeared before a total of 46 different groups with her speech, appropriately titled, "Life With Father—Halsey, That Is."

Instead of an engagement ring, Halsey bought Sula this house at 3149 Ramona in
St. Louis Park in 1922. The address of the house was eventually changed
(to 3231 Alabama) but the Halls remained in this location for 55 years.

Halsey at Home

"Same house, same wife, same suit—must be the gypsy in me."

This expression, voiced often by Halsey, may well sum up the simple approach to life he followed away from the eyes of the public.

Indeed, Halsey did have the same house and wife (although he may actually have possessed more than one suit) for the final 55 years of his life. And, even though he was one of the most widely known personalities in the Twin Cities, for most of this period his name, address, and telephone number were published for all to see in the phone book each year.

"He always said if he was going to be in the public eye, he felt that he owed people his accessibility," his daughter explained.

Eschewing an unlisted number meant a certain amount of inconvenience for Halsey. He heard from many fans who merely wanted an opportunity to talk sports with him for a few minutes. Although most of these conversations took place during reasonable hours, Halsey could count on an occasional post-midnight phone call; in these cases, the callers were most likely a couple of drunks trying to settle a bet before the bars closed and relying on Halsey to answer a sports question for them.

"He'd let them know how mad he was at their waking him up," recalled Sue, "but he'd still give them the answer before hanging up."

One caller Halsey always welcomed, though, was Hubert Humphrey, the Minnesota Senator who also served as vice president of the United States from 1965 to 1969. Through the years, the two had become fast friends; when Humphrey was in Minnesota during the baseball season, he frequently visited Halsey in the broadcast booth. And when Humphrey was back in the nation's capital he often phoned Halsey.

Sue recalled that, during the period Humphrey was vice president, her dad received a phone call from him every Christmas Eve. "I think Hubert was lonely stuck out there in Washington during the holidays," she said. "He just enjoyed calling Daddy and talking baseball with him."

While Halsey's professional career as a speaker, announcer, writer, and referee no doubt kept him busy, he still found plenty of time for a variety of hobbies that took his mind off the world of sports.

One diversion was bridge. The Halls threw lavish bridge parties, according to Sue. During the years that Halsey had his nightly sports show on WCCO Radio, however, he would have to excuse himself for an hour and a half while he drove to the downtown studios and back.

His daughter filled his spot during his absence and, by doing so, also developed a love for the game. Sue reports that, years later, Halsey often returned the favor by filling in when a substitute was needed at her Morningside Bridge club. "There he'd be—the only man among 15 women.

"But he fit right in. The ladies really enjoyed his company, and he enjoyed being with them."

Halsey and Sula enjoyed hosting other types of entertainment besides bridge parties. Sue came up with an invitation her father had had printed for a holiday get-together at the house:

What is loosely known as the opening of the
Holiday Season will take place in the Hall hovel

Sunday, December 19.
Imbibing time: 5:00 p.m. Mastication later for
those who can still pronounce it.

Another passion of Halsey's, at home and on the
road, was soap operas. "He always claimed, all things
considered, that the greatest acting going on in any
media was on the soaps," said Ray Scott. "That's
because every day was a new performance for the
actors on these shows."

During their travels with the Twins, Scott and others became accustomed to Halsey holing up in a hotel
room in the afternoon to watch his soap operas. And
they also knew that disturbing Halsey during these
hours was verboten.

Halsey's favorite soaps were "All My Children,"
"Another World," and "The Edge of Night." Once,
while in New York with the Twins, Halsey even managed to wangle a pass to see the filming of an episode
of "The Edge of Night."

So engrossed with soap operas was Halsey that,
when he and Sula drove to Florida for spring training
every year, they brought along a battery-operated
television. If luck was with them and they were able to
pull in a strong enough signal, the couple would pull
over to the side of the road at one o'clock, hop in the
back seat, and watch their soaps.

Halsey was frequently needled by his friends about
his obsession with soap operas. "He'd tell them, 'It's
just like reading a novel. What's the difference?'" said
Sue, who also picked up her dad's love of these shows.

"We watched the same soap operas and would call
each other during the commercials to discuss what was
going on and what we thought would happen next.

"Sometimes I'd miss a show, and Daddy would fill me

in on what had happened. He'd go into great detail, maintaining the drama of the show. He would even do the voices of all the characters.

"Having Daddy describe what I had missed was better than watching the show in the first place."

Around the house, Halsey was not a handy man, according to Sue. "He was very good with his mouth, but very bad with his hands. When we lived right behind them, Bill would go over and take care of things for him. After we moved to Edina, Pat Harrison from across the street helped him out.

"The only thing he could do well with his hands was play cards and type. Well, he could also make a good drink. But when it came to fix-up jobs, he couldn't change a washer.

"I remember Mother going downstairs once and coming back with the news that the sewer had backed up. Daddy got mad at her for having gone into the basement and seeing this. He told her, 'If you hadn't gone down there, you never would have known the difference.'"

Sue said one of the problems her dad had with fix-up projects was an inability to conceptualize the finished product. "If Mother was making clothes, she'd show him an unfinished portion, but he could never picture the finished dress.

"It was the same thing with work on the house. Since he couldn't picture what the end product would look like, Mother learned that it was best not to tell him when she was going to redecorate. She'd try to schedule the work to be done when he was on a road trip with one of the teams."

One kitchen remodeling project, however, took place while Halsey was at home. Sue said, "He came downstairs one morning and saw a big hole in the middle of the floor. He thought he was having a dream and went back to bed."

According to Sue, her father was "lovable, wonderful, and darling; he just wasn't practical.

"He'd get on a kick of saving money and would make a big deal of turning out all the lights in the house. Then he would eat out of the refrigerator with the door open!"

Perhaps because of the harried lifestyle he led, Halsey appreciated his time at home. "He enjoyed simple pleasures," said Sue. "When he'd get home from his job at the newspaper, he would pick green onions out of the garden, wipe them on his sleeve, and eat them right there. He also loved corn on the cob, and I remember him once eating eight ears in one sitting.

"After learning to play the piano by ear, he fancied himself as quite a musician and once had a fit when Mother tried to give their piano away. Not to worry, though. The stairway was too narrow and they couldn't get it out of the basement.

"Daddy loved parties and having people around him, but he was really a very private person, and he never showed his emotions except when he was happy.

"He was just a genuine, fun-loving, nice, unassuming guy who could never quite believe his success."

Halsey the Poet

"He thought words could solve any problem," said Sue Kennedy of her father.

As a newspaper reporter and columnist for more than forty years, Halsey naturally relied on words in his trade. But his ability as a wordsmith was put to many other uses as well.

Not surprisingly, one of Halsey's favorite ways of conveying encouraging thoughts to family and friends in troubled times was through the written word. The aforementioned letters of support he sent to Gopher football captains over the years are but one example of this proclivity.

Former Minnesota Twins' owner Calvin Griffith also remembers Halsey as a frequent pen pal who often cheered him up. "Halsey kept my morale up during some of the tough times," said Griffith. "He wrote me many encouraging letters and, boy, did I enjoy reading them.

"I've hung on to a lot of the letters and, to this day, whenever I feel low, I go back and read them again."

As often as not, Halsey concluded his letters with a poem, although his poetry turned up in many places other than his personal correspondence. He sometimes inserted a poem in his newspaper column, or he'd scribble a few verses down on any handy scrap of paper; even the back of a placemat could serve as the setting for a poem if the mood to compose struck him during a meal.

"He could write a poem at the drop of a hat," said his daughter, adding that, for Halsey, poetry was sometimes a means of achieving catharsis. "He often used poetry as a way of dealing with problems.

"He might address family difficulties, for instance, with his poems, and, as he recuperated from surgery in 1975, he wrote several poems dealing with that."
The subjects Halsey addressed in his poetry covered a wide spectrum, ranging from sports to soap operas. Most of his poems, however, were directed toward his family.

The remainder of this chapter is devoted to the poetry of Halsey Hall.

Halsey began writing poetry at an early age. He composed the following two poems in February 1910 when he was a few months shy of his twelfth birthday:

Night

The night now comes, all
    still and dark,
Across the meadow, field and
    park.
From out the sky the stars
    doth peep;
And all the world is fast
    asleep.

***

Snowflakes

The snowflakes are falling,
    falling so light
Across the earth, so still and
    white;
One by one, to the earth they fall,
As the north wind roars his
    loud, shrill call.

They are feathery, downy, soft
    and small;
And that is the way the
    snowflakes fall.

* * * * * * * * *

Halsey often included poems about sports stars and events in his newspaper columns, particularly during the early-to-mid 1920s, when he authored a column called "Inside Out" in the St. Paul Pioneer Press.

During the 1920s, the so-called "Golden Age of Sports," there was rarely a shortage of sportwriters eager to supply superlatives over the exploits of immortals such as Red Grange, the "Galloping Ghost," who normally glided across gridirons for the University of Illinois. It was left to Halsey, however, to provide the poetry on the rare occasions when the Ghost stumbled, as was the case in the 1925 season opener versus the Nebraska Cornhuskers:

Red Grange

Stopped in his tracks as cold as death,
    Hardly a chance to draw a breath
Ere the fierce charge of that red wall
    Crushed him to earth with pounding fall.

Pounding the line but all in vain,
    Sweeping the ends without a gain,
Flung to the sod with bruising blow,
    Where is the Grange we used to know?

Hero of Yore but now so low
    Where are the gains he used to show;
Where is the yardage he once reeled;
    Glistening through a broken field?

Able to sprint but not to smash;
    Able to kick but not to crash;
Able to go but not to gain;
    Where is the wonder he shows pain?

Will he come back to us once more;
    Has the world fame for him in store?
Flaming-haired star that used to be
    Come back to us and gallop free.

***

*Babe Ruth's errant behavior turned the 1925 season
into a nightmare for him and his Yankee teammates
and finally caused him to be suspended by manager
Miller Huggins in late August. Halsey addressed the
Babe's wayward habits with this poem that appeared in
his column September 1, 1925:*

Fandom to the Babe

Is it goodbye, Babe, forever say,
Or will you come back to us some day
With your home run swat and winning smile
As you clout the ball in your famous style?

Can't you drop the ways that lead you off
To the realm where people only scoff;
Where they jeer at you instead of cheer
And forget that you to Fame were dear.

Where the loud guffaw will be your share
And the merry razz will fill the air,
As the people all forget the praise,
That they gave to you in your palmy days.

So come back to us, we're asking you,
Let us see again that follow through
As you put your weight behind the smash
That had made you great before your crash.

***

*On the October 1925 passing of pitching great Christy
Mathewson, a victim of tuberculosis:*

Matty

Oh Big Six, have you heard the call
Of the Great Umpire over all?
Have you released the earthly curve
A better land to love and serve?

It was a gallant fight you made;
You fought it well and unafraid;
To meet the end we all must meet
You fought it well without retreat.

All fandom's honors silent stand
Before you, loved by all the land.
Your name was spotless, stainless, white.
It stays forever on the height.

The robe of greatness cloaked your frame,
Your leaving rends your much-loved game,
When mem'ry paints your features fair;
'Twill put a baseball halo there.

***

*A paean to the hockey team of the St. Paul Athletic
Club:*

In Review

Do you recall in days of old
The Moose's charge when nights were cold;
The threat of Stewart's speed and grace,
Where centers failed to match his pace?

The days when Goodman really flashed,
When Conacher and Seaborn clashed,
When Bonney, of the Pittsburgh clan,
Would make a foe an also ran?

When Drury of the speeding skate
Burned icy paths with blist'ring gait;
Fitzgerald, not a pilot then,
Ranked first among the defense men?

The day when Saintly colors flew;
Far flung to breezes for the view
Of teams that ranked far down the line
From where the A. C. used to shine.

When St. Paul ruled as hockey's best
To lead its rivals from the West?
But grieve not that they triumphed then
When there is chance to start again.

***

On the excitement of an inside-the-park home run:

The Inside Homer

There are clouts that please the eye
As they sail away so high
On their journey o'er the far and distant wall;
But the swat at which to bark
Is the one inside the park
Where the runner has to slide to beat the ball.

***

Other offerings from his "Inside Out" Column:

Ain't it the Truth?

He jeered the umpire loudly
      And wished he'd go to grass;
He razzed the struggling pitcher
      And said his arm was glass;
He knew as much of baseball
      As a simple country lass
And yet he led the hooting
      For he got in on a pass.

***

Do You Blame Him?

"You are out!" the umpire shouted,
      As he waved his arm aside,
"You are right," the player answered,
      And the ump fell back and died.

141

***

The Suicide

He stood on the bridge at midnight
   And longed for the nerve to jump,
He'd thrown in the groove to Hornsby
   And called Tyrus Cobb a chump.

***

Strong But Stupid

His name was Socko Simpson and his fielding was immense
   And when it came to hitting he could sock them o'er the fence
A tearing, sliding runner, he made rival basemen mind,
   But when it came to thinking he was like a melon rind.

There wasn't much he could not do to speed and twisting curve
   His bat rang out the curfew for a foeman pitcher's nerve;
He weighed a mere two hundred pounds and every ounce of strength
   Was concentrated in his swing which made home runs of length.

His uniform was natty and he always kept it pressed
   In fact it was a wonder that he did not wear a vest;
His shoes were always shined up bright as also was his hair,
   But when it came to thinking, well, he simply wasn't there.

He thrilled the fans with catches that it seemed he could not make
   He made the rival pitcher look as soft as mother's cake;
But of what value was his skill when in a crucial place
   He tried to purloin second with a pal upon the base?

***

The player grabbed the bounding ball
  And rushed it toward the goal;
He pushed his foemen right and left
  And opened up a hole;
And when he crossed the final line,
  Awaiting fame's loud call;
He heard instead a roar of jeers;
  For this was basketball.

***

The Smart Veteran

They called him the luckiest guy in the world
  With only a prayer and a glove
But he managed to win all his games quite at ease
  Which is just what the home rooters love.

He was slow, fat, and forty with only a ghost
  Of his fast ball that once used to flash,
But the mightiest hitters, when facing his craft,
  Saw their batting percentage go smash.

With a corkscrewy twist that he'd practiced for years
  He would float the old sphere to the plate
You could count all the seams on the slow-moving ball
  Try to hit it, you'd always be late.

You ask what was the secret of how he could win
  Good control is the heart of it all;
There is many a hero with plenty of brains
  Who hasn't a thing on the ball.

***

A Basketball Player

Give me the pivot that baffles the guard,
Give me the dribble that's owned by the starred;
Give me the feint and a sidestep or two,
Give me the eye that will send the ball through.

***

At the Rassling Match

Twelve thousand fans yelled loudly
　　To see the wrestlers roll
They loved to watch the athletes;
　　It pleased their very soul;
But when the match was over
　　And they were 'neath the sky;
You asked them why they liked it;
　　They could not tell you why.

***

The Wrestler

Slam him down upon his face,
　　Jump upon his spine;
Make his blood run fast and free,
　　Cut his features fine;
Grunt and groan and grunt some more,
　　Crash a few ribs in;
But, remember, lose the match,
　　It's not your turn to win.

***

This lament to the passing of Nicollet Park and its renowned right-field fence appeared in the <u>Minneapolis Star</u> *in 1955. In it, Halsey pays homage to some of the Miller sluggers who sent home runs over the fence, including Hall-of-Famer Ted Williams, who spent the 1938 season in Minneapolis before moving up to the Boston Red Sox.*

> Gone is the home of musclemen,
>   Gone to the wrecker's crew;
> Gone is the land of Hauser and Buzz,
>   That right-field fence is through.
>
> London Bridge may be toppling again
>   And Humpty Dumpty may fall;
> But never again will Wilson punch
>   Over that right-field wall.
>
> Gavvy and Clymer, Harris and Gill
>   homered for many a score;
> Williams, the great, paced a slugging gait
>   Over the fence that's no more.
>
> Only the rubble and memories,
>   Of the land of slug renown,
> Are lying out there in Nicollet's snow;
>   That right-field fence is down.

* * * * * * * * *

Halsey was most prolific as a poet, however, when the inspiration was his family. To his grandchildren, Billy, Kathy, and Cindy:

My Billy

Boy of mine, where do you roam,
What, or where, do you call your home?
Manhood awaits you, don't you know that?
Well, pick up a ball and pick up a bat.

Whack out to the future a line drive or two,
You'll get whatever is coming to you,
But come it will not if favor you give
To a few who care not however they live.

We love you, dear boy, past your fartherest dreams,
Out there where the glimmer of future life beams,
Your parents may pitch and your sisters may catch
But errors may trap you and cause a mismatch.

So pick up the cudgel of life and swing wide
You'll swing and you'll swing until God's on your side
And then all the problems will fall into place
And life will be happy with hopes you can face.

***

My Kathy

There are times I think of, Kappy Dear,
When you were born just yesteryear:
When Grandma called, her voice awhirl,
She cried, "You have a baby girl."

She cried with laughter in her eyes,
As though she'd seen God through the skies.

I was in Melbourne, far away,
And yet it seemed a wondrous day:

Because we'd gained a girl so true
That o'er our sorrows joy broke through.

So now you're graduating, dear,
Into a world that has its fear,
But this old world should sit at ease
Because our Kappy all will please.

***

To Cindy, birthday, 1972

When the angels sing in Heaven, their notes are clear
  and clean,
And the song they sing most often is known as sweet 16;
They'll sing it now to Cindy, whose being we adore,
Though 16 is the number, we hope there're 80 more.

***

To My Children

Do you know the most wonderful thing I own?
It occurs to me often when I am alone;
It's Billy and Kathy and Cindy so dear
You brighten the sunshine whenever you're near.

You play well together and play well alone,
You worship our GOD and ne'er cast a stone
At HIS ten commandments we all must obey;
You smile and you laugh as you travel your way.

You've worked and you've learned and bettered yourselves
E'er since the old days when you were just elves.

I pray that forever so happy you'll be;
That is my fondest wish for my Lovable Three.

* * * * *

To his son-in-law, Bill (written for Bill's 52nd birthday on November 30, 1977, this was the last poem Halsey ever wrote):

It doesn't really matter that you're hitting 52,
Especially when it happens to a dandy guy like you;
You've been an OK fellow since the day that you were born,
So just to help you celebrate, please take this quart of corn!

* * * * *

To his daughter, Sue:

Suzanne

There was a time when you were one,
And now you've grown to forty-one;
And always, dear, along the way,
We've never heard your sweet lips say
An unkind word to Mom or Dad,
Oh, what a happy life we've had.
                                    May 18, 1968

***

So now you've reached the age of fifty;
We s'pose you think that's rather nifty;

To tell the truth, my sweetheart Sue,
That's just what we were thinking, too.

The years have flown on wings so fast.
The laughs and tears have come and passed;
Through many a sun and many a cloud,
You've held your poise and love so proud.

The joys that spring from the womb or time
Have made your life and ours sublime;
A half a century of love
We share with you from God above.

Papa
May 18, 1977

* * * * *

And, finally, to his wife, Sula:

One Year

A year of joy,
A year of cheer,
A year of sorrows dead,
A year of jokes,
A year of fun,
Has passed since we were wed.

A year of toil,
A year of work,
Since we took marriage vow,
A year of cares,
A year of frowns,
Yet I would not change now.

A year of love,
A year of hugs,
With many kisses sweet,
A year of looks,
A year of thrills,
From shoulders to our feet.

A year of hopes,
A year of bliss,
Why wonder that I laugh,
A year of thought,
A year of prayer,
From cups of joy I quaff.

                    December 20, 1923

                    ***

I want to sit on the dav with you
    And watch our soaps go by;
I want to sit and hold your hand
    And sometimes laugh or cry.
But the main thing is, my sweetheart dear,
    If the plots be false or true,
It mattereth not what fun they are
    As long as I'm with you.

***

Twas many years ago, my dear, in the halls of Old Duluth,
When you and I, both at that time, enjoyed the glow of youth;
I'd anoint your brow with kisses and stroke your raven hair
And always I'd feel better just to have you sitting there.

The years have passed, my darling, and, with the passing
    years,
Has come the full contentment that can banish all our fears;
I hold you close too seldom, my sweetheart and my wife,
But bless the day our Savior brought you into my life.

And then you gave us Toodie, who's been a wondrous joy;
And she, in turn, gave us two girls as well as Billy boy;
You've done your work, but still you work for days that never
    end;
I think, when summing up is done, God's blessings He will
    send.

I've shirked the bills and mussed the house and caused you
    much distress,
But, through it all, you've stayed with me and brought much
    happiness;
The peonies and iris, they would wither on the vine,
If ever I should see the day when you're no longer mine.

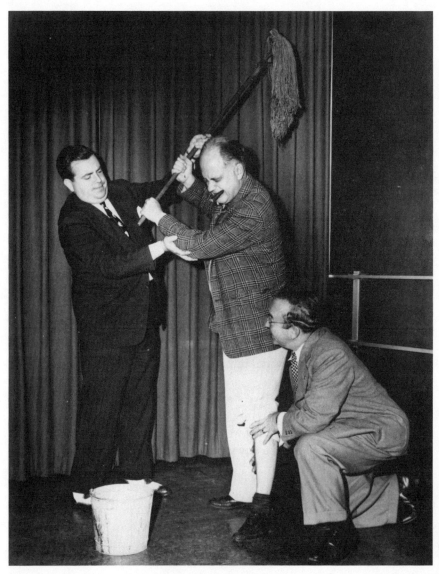

Halsey hams it up with broadcast colleague Paul Wann (left) and Charlie Johnson, his boss at the <u>Minneapolis Star</u>.

Halsey the Character

"The premier writers of our day—Dick Cullum, George Edmond, Ed Shave—were quite a bunch of characters," said St. Paul sports columnist Don Riley. "But Halsey could out-character all of them."

"He definitely liked being an individualist," agreed Norene Heine Becker. Becker, the granddaughter of Halsey's sister-in-law Katie Marcks, recalls Halsey once using mustard as a topping for his ice cream. "I don't think he particularly liked the concoction," she added. "He just did it to be different and to call attention to himself."

Indeed, Halsey was never at a loss for traits that caused him to stand out. He had a laugh so contagious, legend has it, that traveling vaudeville companies used to hire him as a one-man claque for opening nights.

His many idiosyncracies, along with a great sense of humor, made him a frequent target—albeit a willing one—of his friends' wisecracks.

When Herb Carneal was unable to attend a dinner in 1975 honoring his former partner, he sent along this letter which was read to the group:

First, Halsey, just a brief explanation as to my absence. You see, I had to choose between either being at your party or accepting an invitation to be a judge in the All-World Halitosis Contest. The sponsors of the Halitosis Contest felt that, having worked with you for eleven years with your cigars, garlic, and onions, I was extremely well-qualified to be a judge.

When I first joined you and Ray Scott as a

member of the Twins' broadcasting team in 1962, I was amazed at what good health you were in. The only defect you seemed to have was an apparent kidney problem. You never said anything about this, but I noticed that whenever we'd go out to eat and you'd see the waiter coming with the check, you'd have to go to the men's room.

One fact should be brought out, though. Since you haven't been on the Twins broadcasts, attendance at the games has declined considerably. The reason should be obvious; when you were announcing the games, people had to come out to the ball park to find out what was really going on.

Halsey, you were in the broadcast business for over 50 years, and, in the time that I've known you, I do want folks to know I think you're one of the most humble men I've ever met. But let's face it, Halsey, you've got a lot to be humble about.

> *Your long-suffering sidekick,*
> *Herb Carneal*

The audience roared with laughter as Howard Viken, the master of ceremonies, read Carneal's letter; no one, however, laughed harder than Halsey.

"He loved being picked on like that," said Riley. "He could go along with a gag beautifully."

Another colleague, Dick Cullum, instigated many jokes at Halsey's expense. "Cullum had a real pixie streak in him," said sports historian Stan Carlson. "He especially loved pulling tricks on Halsey."

One such prank occurred in Iowa City during a trip to cover a Gopher football game against the Iowa Hawkeyes. Members of the press stayed at a hotel that was hosting a women's convention at the time. The guest rooms opened onto a circular balcony that overlooked the lobby.

The day before the game, several of the writers gathered in Cullum's room for cocktails. Lounging in a chair with a drink in his hand, a half-dressed Halsey asked where the bathroom was. With a wink to the others in the room, Cullum pointed to the door leading to the hall.

According to one witness, Halsey breezed out of the room and shut the door behind him before realizing he was on a balcony, in full view of several hundred women, clad only in his underwear.

Halsey smiled and waved to the ladies before going back in the room.

Another story involving Cullum and Halsey took place on a fateful Gopher football trip to Seattle in 1936. The team and media members traveled by train for their season opener against the Washington Huskies and stayed overnight in Missoula, Montana, the Wednesday before that Saturday's game.

Most of the entourage was quartered at the Florence Hotel, which caught fire at around four o'clock in the morning. The hero of the journey was *St. Paul Daily News* sports editor Ed Shave, who was returning from a night on the town when he saw smoke billowing out of the building.

Shave rushed inside and shouted to the night clerk, "Your hotel's on fire!"

"Go to bed," mumbled the clerk. "You're drunk."

"That may be," slurred Shave, "but your hotel's still on fire."

The hotel was completely gutted by the blaze, but thanks to Shave's nocturnal prowling an alarm was sounded in time for the guests and residents to escape.

Several of the Gophers were treated for smoke inhalation, but the chief harm of the fire, according to head coach Bernie Bierman, was the loss of sleep it caused his players.

The Gopher contingent arrived safely in Seattle Friday afternoon and checked into the Olympic Hotel. Rollie Johnson, an announcer for WCCO, said that Cullum, Halsey, and he planned on going to dinner that evening with Sheila Carter, a former news reporter at WTCN Radio in Minneapolis who by this time was working at a station in Seattle.

Carter joined the trio in the room Cullum and Halsey shared on the 15th floor. Johnson recalls that, as they waited for Halsey to finish showering (apparently this time Cullum had given him correct directions to the bathroom), Cullum spotted Halsey's shoes on the floor near the window.

"For no particular reason," said Johnson, "Dick bent over, picked up the shoes, and blithely tossed them out the window. When Halsey got out of the shower, he started getting dressed, but, of course, he couldn't find his shoes.

"As Cullum urged him to hurry, saying we'd be late for our dinner reservations, Halsey searched everywhere. Finally Dick said, 'Halsey, I remember now. You didn't have your shoes on when we left Missoula. They must have burned up in the fire.'"

The explanation was good enough for Halsey, who grabbed his coat and took off in his stocking feet. Johnson says no one in the crowded elevator noticed that Halsey was without his shoes. "When we hit the street, though, a burly cab driver noticed Halsey, grabbed him by his lapels, and said, 'Hey, Buddy. Are these your shoes?'

"Halsey, in his usual style, said, 'Well now, my good

man, they are, and pray tell where did you find them?'

"The driver replied, 'They landed on top of my cab and damn near went through the roof.'"

Johnson says the escapade concluded when they told the driver that Sheila Carter had inadvertently knocked the shoes off the window ledge and assured him that her radio station would pay for the damage to the cab.

These weren't the only incidents in which Halsey, literally or figuratively, was caught with his pants down.

Fellow *Tribune* reporter Tom Briere says that Halsey arrived at Spring Training with the Millers one year after having lost a considerable amount of weight over the winter. "He didn't have a belt to fit, so he used a piece of rope instead," said Briere. "As he was getting out of the car in front of a fashionable restaurant, though, the rope broke.

"Halsey managed to grab his pants at half mast."

Halsey's colleagues report that he seemed to have a knack for finding himself in such unusual situations. "Strange things like that were always happening to him," said former Gopher football coach Murray Warmath. "He was laughing all the time. And if others weren't picking at him, he'd be running around trying to stir something up himself."

"He was always performing one way or another," added Briere. "The man was a born entertainer."

Many of the stories about Halsey revolve around common themes such as his great disdain for air travel and his equally-strong love of distilled beverages.

Halsey's behavior as a character, though, may not always have been a true reflection of him, but rather a part of an image he tried to project.

To a certain extent, he was playing a part. For

example, while he always requested (demanded, actually) separate checks in a restaurant and liked to feign stinginess, à la Jack Benny, he was, in reality, an extremely giving person. (Allan Holbert of the *Minneapolis Tribune* once wrote, "Halsey's so generous that he used to give a buck to anyone who would walk in off the street with a hard luck story. Once one old-timer sent Halsey a letter saying he couldn't make it in for his dole that week and asking him to mail it to him instead. Halsey, needless to say, complied.")

No doubt Halsey did genuinely love to drink, although he often imbibed as a means of promoting his persona as a bon vivant. Colleagues also steadfastly maintain that he never allowed his drinking to interfere with his work.

"He just liked to drink," said Ray Scott. "Some of it may have been his way of emulating W. C. Fields, his favorite comedian. He imitated Fields in many ways, particularly in his manner of addressing me as 'Scottie, my boy.'"

Scott added that, while it was probably inadvertent, Halsey took on many of his hero's speech mannerisms. "When Halsey was talking, you could close your eyes and swear it was W. C. Fields."

A hallmark of Halsey's on Twins' road trips was a satchel full of liquor bottles that he toted with him. "If anyone ever asked about the contents of that satchel," said Dave Mona, who covered the Twins for the *Minneapolis Tribune* in the 1960s, "he would merely say that it contained reference books.

"If that was the case, they were the only reference books I ever knew of that clinked."

"He had so many bottles in that bag of his," added Joe Soucheray, "that when he stepped off a plane, he sounded like a glockenspiel."

One of Halsey's most memorable lines came in response to a question from a young reporter about his reason for lugging a satchel of liquor from town to town. "After all," said the reporter, "every city we go to has a bar in it."

"My boy," Halsey replied, "you never know when you'll run into a local election."

Halsey usually restocked his satchel during the course of a trip, taking advantage of cut-rate liquor stores in several of the cities he visited. His favorites were Central Liquor in Washington, D.C. and Zimmerman's in Chicago. Halsey, it was reported, was not averse to forking over five dollars in cab fare to find a bargain on booze.

Nor was Halsey reluctant to find other ways to save on the cost of a drink. Ray Scott remembers a dinner at the Eager House in Baltimore when Halsey had a flask filled with gin tucked away in his pocket. "When the waiter came around the first time, Halsey ordered a gin and tonic," said Scott. "After a while the waiter came by to see if we wanted another round. The rest of us ordered another drink, but Halsey said, 'No thank you.' This continued. What the waiter didn't know was that, as soon as he left the table, Halsey would take out his flask and refill his glass.

"Eventually the waiter became suspicious. Finally, as he left the table he took a few steps and whirled around. But Halsey had been watching him like a hawk. As soon as the waiter turned expecting to catch him with his flask, Halsey just smiled and slowly waved at him.

"It was a game with Halsey."

Former Twins' media relations director Tom Mee recalls another trip to Baltimore when Howard Fox, the team's traveling secretary, invited a dozen members of the press to dinner at the Chesapeake Restaurant. "Halsey ordered a drink—a scotch and water—before dinner," said Mee, "but that was it. He just refilled his drink from his flask and kept turning down the waitress when she'd come by and ask if he wanted another.

"Finally Halsey turned to Bob Wolff, one of the other announcers, and asked, 'How much do you think this will cost?'

"'What do you care?' Wolff said. 'Fox is picking up the tab.'

"Halsey was so mad that he hadn't found that out earlier. All this time he was going through the scotch in his flask and turning down the drink offers."

Halsey apparently wasn't the only person who looked for ways to save money on liquor, according to his daughter Sue. "Mother and Daddy had one set of friends who never served liquor at their home but would drink like fish when they came to one of my parents' parties.

"In fact, they were so cheap that one time Daddy caught them in the kitchen pouring his liquor into a bottle to take home."

Despite the fondness he exhibited for alcohol throughout most of his adult life, Halsey didn't drink until he was 28 years old. He credits (or blames) his boss at the *Minneapolis Journal*, sports editor John McGovern, with introducing him to bathtub gin in 1926.

"He was never a beer drinker," said Sue. "He didn't care much for bourbon, either. For Daddy, it was mostly scotch or gin."

Regardless of what type of libation may have been available, Halsey was always in the mood for a party. He particularly enjoyed late afternoon get-togethers—called "Hawthornes"—in someone's hotel room following a game at spring training.

"For us, a Hawthorne was a good, old-fashioned party," explained Frank Buetel, who broadcast games for both the Millers and Twins. "We felt that giving our happy hours such a name added a bit of class."

Jimmy Byrne of the *Minneapolis Star* said that Halsey could be seen at his craziest at these affairs. Byrne remembers Halsey once arriving at a Hawthorne alone and explaining that Sula would join him shortly. "A few minutes later the phone rang," said Byrne. "It was Sula calling for Halsey. After muttering 'Yes' a couple of times, Halsey said, 'Well, why don't you call a bellboy?' and hung up.

"When we asked him what that was all about, he said, 'Sula wanted me to come back and zip up her dress for her. I told her to call a bellboy instead.'

"Halsey wouldn't let anything interfere with a Hawthorne."

Corresponding closely with Halsey's love of drinking was his fear of flying. Halsey's intake of "flight medicine," as he called it, increased in concert with his anxieties prior to takeoff.

"Halsey was the only man I know who was at 10,000 feet before the plane even took off," said Ray Scott, adding that he sometimes kidded Halsey that his fear of air travel was a hoax and that he just used this phobia as an excuse to drink.

Dick Gordon recalls sitting next to Halsey on one of his first flights. "As the pilot revved the engine, Halsey sat there with his eyes closed and his hands trembling. After a few minutes he turned and stammered, 'Are we there yet?'

"We hadn't even left the ground."

No matter how many times he flew, Halsey never became a fan of this form of travel. Nor did he endear himself to airline clerks when he would approach the ticket counter and ask for "One chance to Chicago."

Some of the stories centering on Halsey's fear of flying may be apocryphal, but a few are good enough to bear repeating anyway, such as the time he attempted to get from Minneapolis to Bloomington, Indiana without flying. He took a train to Indianapolis and then tried to rent an automobile. He couldn't find his driver's license, however, and ended up having to drive around the block and pass an Indiana driving exam before being allowed to rent the car.

On another occasion he spent three days, via train and car, getting to and from a speaking engagement in Decorah, Iowa, when he could have made the round trip by plane in a few hours.

But no matter how much longer it made the journey, Halsey traveled by train whenever possible.

"It wasn't just a matter of trying to avoid flying," said his daughter. "Daddy just loved trains. If he hadn't become a writer and a sports announcer, he probably would have been a conductor on a train."

"My wife Kay was the manager of World Wide Travel at the Auto Club," said Norm McGrew. "Halsey would spend hours at Kay's desk, studying those train schedules to see if it would be possible to get to his destination by rail instead of air."

But rail travel was not always feasible, so like it or not, Halsey had to take to the air. Sue Kennedy said that the antics of her father's friends didn't help to soothe his anxieties. "Before one flight, they arranged to have the pilot wear dark glasses and walk past Daddy with a Seeing Eye dog."

Glenn Gostick, a man connected with the local sports scene in many ways, remembered Gopher hockey coach John Mariucci trying to be philosophical with

Halsey on the subject. "As they boarded the plane," recalled Gostick, "Mariucci said to him, 'Don't fret about it, Halsey. After all, when it's your time to go, it's your time to go.'

" 'Yeah,' replied Halsey. 'But what if it's the pilot's time to go?' "

Paul Giel recalled a certain flight on which he sat next to Halsey. "Shortly after takeoff, they started passing out the salads," said Giel. "Halsey had braced himself with a few nips out of his flask and didn't notice that the cellophane was still wrapped over the salad. He started sprinkling the salad dressing on top of the cellophane and poking his fork through it.

"Finally he noticed something was wrong so he called the stewardess over and asked, 'Since when did you start putting condoms over your salads?' "

Of course, many of Halsey's cohorts maintain that traveling with him was always an adventure—in the air or on the ground.

Herb Carneal related another incident that occurred at the Eager House in Baltimore during dinner with Halsey and Merle Harmon, who had replaced Scott on the Twins' broadcasts following the 1966 season. "The three of us had our own table, while Howard Fox was in a nearby booth with some friends of his. We saw Fox gesturing toward us on one occasion, probably pointing out the team's broadcasters—with some pride, we hoped—to his friends.

"When we finished eating, the check was delivered and Halsey was taken aback by the total. He called the waiter back over and asked him to re-add the figures. 'What are you trying to do?' he said. 'Put the chef on a pension?'

"The waiter pulled out his pencil, did a little addition, and said, 'No sir, this is the correct amount.'

"If that wasn't enough, Halsey then reached into his pocket for his wallet and discovered it wasn't there. He probably had left it back at the hotel, but the combination of events was too much for Halsey. Before we could stop him, he stood up and began tapping his water glass with his spoon.

"'Ladies and gentlemen,' he announced to the patrons, including Fox who looked like he wanted to crawl under his table and hide, 'I want you to know that this is the biggest clip joint I've ever been in.

"'Not only do they pad the check, but they also pick your pocket!'"

Ray Scott said when they were in the nation's capital, they often dined at Duke Zeibert's restaurant. "Duke Zeibert's was a hangout for a lot of the Washington bigshots—cabinet officials, administration people, sports figures," Scott explained. "Some people referred to Duke as the Toots Shor of Washington. He'd always correct them and say, 'No, Toots is the Duke Zeibert of New York.'

"Duke was a fellow with a great flair about him, and he loved Halsey. He'd always say of him, 'There's the last of a dying breed—the old-time newspaper man.'

"We went to Duke's for dinner shortly after I joined the Twins' broadcast crew. Halsey had some other business to tend to first, so he said he'd meet me there. It was a Saturday night and the place was crowded.

"I was waiting at the bar when I saw Halsey walk in the front door. Now, consider that Halsey was never too resplendent in his dress to begin with. Everything he had was rather baggy and, traveling as he did, his suits were sometimes a bit rumpled. This sort of thing never bothered Halsey, though, and, on more than one occasion, he'd be wearing a necktie with bits of several days' worth of breakfast and lunch clinging to it.

"This would probably accurately describe Halsey's attire that evening. In addition, he had obviously had a few drinks before departing and arrived with a real glow.

"This very officious maître d' took one look at Halsey and decided he wanted no part of him. I was watching the whole thing from the bar, wondering what was going to happen.

"Just as I was about to rescue Halsey, Duke Zeibert spotted what was going on and headed over there. About halfway across the dining room, Duke threw out his arms and said, 'Halsey, how are you?'

"I'll always remember the way Halsey turned to the maître d' with a look that seemed to say, 'Take that, you peasant.'

"He had such a look of triumph on his face."

On another trip to Washington, D.C. the group skipped Duke Zeibert's and ended up at an Italian restaurant instead. "There were four of us—a couple of the Minneapolis writers, Halsey, and me," said Scott. "We had all had a few drinks before we got there and must have looked a bit scruffy because the maître d' decided the perfect place for us was in one of the back dining rooms where it was quite dark.

"After our eyes adjusted to the dim lights, we looked around and saw a young couple at a nearby booth. It was obvious he was giving her the big pitch and expecting great things from this evening. Just then, a violinist and a tenor walked into the room and were summoned to the booth where they serenaded the couple.

"After the musicians finished playing for the couple, they made a terrible mistake. They walked over to our table. Right away, Halsey could smell a tip, so he took it upon himself to act as our spokesman.

"When the tenor asked if he could sing something for us, Halsey said, 'No, my good man. I believe we heard your entire repertoire when you were back at that booth.'

"The man then made his second mistake. He pressed on. Halsey looked him in the eye and said, 'You know, I've always been suspicious of anyone with a voice as high as yours.'

"That dispensed with the music."

During his tenure with the Twins, Scott spent a great deal of time with Halsey, and maintains that he often tried to watch over him on road trips. "Halsey was such a trusting soul that he could never understand why it wasn't safe to go into certain spots of some cities. He'd sometimes go berserk over the prices a hotel restaurant or bar would charge for drinks and would want to walk to a cheaper place. I wouldn't want him walking the streets at night and would at least insist that we take a cab."

Scott recalls a particular cab ride through lower Manhattan with a driver who liked to talk. "All the way from our hotel down to the financial district, the driver was pointing out the birthplaces of prominent people. 'So-and-so was born on this street,' he'd tell us.

"Finally, Halsey had enough and said, 'I'll bet you don't know who was born down this street,' he said.

"The cab driver said, 'Well, sir, knowing as much as I do about New York, I can assure you it was no one important.'

"'I beg your pardon,' Halsey replied in an indignant tone. 'I was born on that street.'"

Halsey, it seemed, would go most anywhere and do most anything in the interest of a good deal on a drink, and he displayed the same zeal when it came to food.

Frank Buetel, who worked with Halsey on the Twins'

television broadcasts in the early 1970s, said that fabulous postgame meals were served in the press rooms of most of the stadiums in the league. "Halsey would always make the most of these free meals. Not only that, but he would charm the daylights out of the ladies who prepared and served the food. They just loved him and would make sure he didn't go away empty-handed.

"By the time we'd leave the ball park, Halsey would have a brown bag loaded with sandwiches and pickles and chips."

For Halsey, the next-best thing to a free meal was one at which he could at least receive a separate check.

"He wasn't always popular with waitresses because they would prefer to write out just one check for the entire group," said Sue Kennedy. "But Daddy would be persistent about it.

"Once, in Kansas City when we joined Daddy on a Twins' road trip, he really got into it with the waitress. I remember him finally blurting out, 'I'll buy you a whole damn pad of those things if you'll just give us separate checks.' She never did, though. The waitress won this time."

Ray Scott recalls a similar situation while dining with Halsey at Toots Shor's in New York. "We ordered a few drinks and had dinner. The waiter then came by and handed us one check for the two of us. Halsey reminded him that he had requested separate checks. The waiter gave him a patronizing look and informed him this wasn't possible.

"Halsey then summoned the most sarcastic tone of voice he was capable of and said, 'Shortage of paper in this great city?'"

Halsey's most distinctive trademarks, however, may have been his love of cigars and green onions.

Knowing this, many fans sent Halsey fine imported cigars, but, much to the displeasure of his comrades, he al-ways preferred the cheaper variety.

An even greater bane to those he shared a press box with may have been his copious consumption of green onions. Halsey swore by the health effects of these pungent scallions, however.

"In all his years with the newspaper and radio, he never missed a day of work due to illness," said his daughter, "and he always credited onions for his good health."

"They combat many ailments and inhibit cholesterol," he once testified. "I eat both green and bulb onions with and between meals."

Life with Halsey Hall was memorable and anything but boring, his colleagues agree, adding that Halsey—in many different ways—made an impact wherever he went.

"There was never a dull moment with Halsey around," said Jules Perlt.

"To work and travel with Halsey as I did was an experience shared by a precious few," said Stew MacPherson, who broadcast Gopher football with Halsey in the 1950s. "And to have survived all those years with him was nothing short of a bloody miracle."

"Halsey laughed his way through life, and he kept the rest of us laughing, too," added Dick Cullum.

Twin Cities sports columnist Patrick Reusse summed up the matter with this observation: "Halsey wrote about characters, but he was a better one himself."

Ho Ho Holy Cow!

He didn't keep it for long, but a hirsute Halsey once sported a moustache.

Although he was never known for his sartorial splendor, Halsey at times could be downright dapper.

Halsey prepare a dose of "flight medicine" for colleague Herb Carneal.

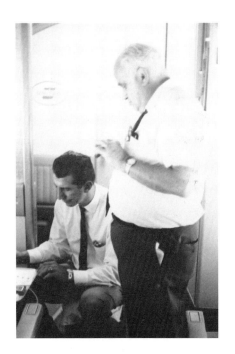

Alongside his favorite form of travel.

On board a flight, Halsey passes the time with Twins' coach Billy Martin.

Halsey and Sula in front of the "It's a Small, Small World" ride, their favorite attraction at Walt Disney World.

A determined-looking Halsey watches the barbecue in 1973.

For several years, Halsey and Sula served as tour leaders on Caribbean cruises.

The Many Sides of Halsey Hall

Although he was once described by television news-
caster Dave Moore as a "reliable repository of encyclo-
pedic baseball knowledge", Halsey Hall had many
other interests and could converse intelligently on a
variety of subjects far beyond the world of sports.

"He wasn't all baseball," said Don Riley. "He could
talk on history or European affairs. Few people knew
how well-traveled he was.

"What made him such a well-rounded person was his
ability to talk about most everything."

Halsey had the chance to do just that in the late
1950s, when he had a half-hour television show that
appeared on WCCO-TV every Friday night at 10:30. A
promotional blurb written by the sponsor, Twin City
Federal Saving & Loan, described the "Halsey Hall
Show" in this manner:

> "This locally produced 'conversation' show is a
> counterpart of the New York and network programs
> which have attained a vogue. Halsey Hall, who
> fronts it, is the dean of newspaper and radio sports-
> writers and sportscasters and the local George
> Jessel of the banquet merry-go-round.
>
> "Hall boasts a host of friends and followers who
> have been attracted by his amiability, wit, and
> generally endearing qualities. He easily is the
> community's most popular and sought after emcee
> and toastmaster...
>
> "In his own video show Hall largely departs from
> sports and, instead, comments, philosophizes, and
> reminisces gently anent a wide variety of subjects,
> tossing in some jokes and gags for good measure. He
> does it well."

Halsey also demonstrated his versatility as a panelist on "Mind Over Microphone," a WCCO Radio quiz show hosted by E. W. Ziebarth. Often he would outshine the show's designated intellectuals.

"Halsey was a regular on the show and he was superb," said Ziebarth. "He simply could not be matched in terms of his memory of sports events of the past. He also demonstrated a good knowledge of other subject matter and, indeed, that's what made him spectacular.

"I recall once having the dean of one of the graduate schools at the University of Minnesota as a panelist on the show. There was a subtle and little-known aspect of Shakespearean literature on which I asked a question. The dean, whom I admire enormously, was unable to respond, but Halsey did.

"He would astound people because they didn't expect him to have any knowledge of these types of things."

While baseball, football, basketball, and hockey games may have dominated his schedule, Halsey always found time to take part in other activities. He and Sula served as judges for the Miss Minnesota beauty contest during the years it was staged at the Excelsior Amusement Park ballroom. They were there in 1948, the year BeBe Shopp won the pageant en route to becoming the first Minnesotan to be crowned Miss America.

Halsey and Sula also loved attending the theater. Don Stolz, owner of the Old Log Theater, said the Halls were frequent visitors at his playhouse and recalls how much he enjoyed them. "It was a joy having them here. The audience was delighted when I would introduce Halsey from the stage. He was a much-loved man.

"Back in those days, we did a new show at the Old

Log every two weeks, so the Halls were here quite often. As we did so often with other members of the press, we liked to give them complimentary tickets.

"Halsey always objected to getting the tickets for free, but we always managed to get them to him. After a while, it became a game between us. He was determined to pay for the tickets, so he'd try subterfuges of various types, like making the reservations in his daughter's name. Our people in the box office caught on, though, and would leave the complimentary tickets.

"He never was successful in paying for the tickets. But he always *wanted* to; that was the difference."

Halsey and Sula enjoyed traveling, although the baseball season normally precluded a vacation during the summer. Instead, they often squeezed in a trip just prior to the opening of spring training.

For many years, the Halls took a train south a few weeks before the start of the Grapefruit League games and served as tour leaders on Caribbean cruises sponsored by the American Automobile Association (AAA) of Minneapolis. "We often used Halsey as a tour leader to entice people to take the cruises," said Dennis Blenis of the AAA. "I was impressed by the effort he put into it. Halsey would study the guest list before the trip to become familiar with the names. By doing that, he reached the point on the cruise where he could call nearly all the guests by name."

"It was surprising, though, that as much as he liked people, he wasn't all that comfortable as a host. He had a shy side and didn't like to push himself on people. He loved talking to the guests, but sometimes had trouble approaching them. I'd tell the people on the cruise to go talk to him. 'Halsey really wants to talk to you,' I'd tell them. And he did."

In the spring of 1957, the Halls took the *Queen Mary* to London for the beginning of a European vacation. Halsey combined business with pleasure by writing a series of articles about the trip that appeared in the *Minneapolis Star.* The first report described the voyage across the rough waters of the Atlantic Ocean:

LONDON—When did you last see an indoor swimming pool with two-foot waves?

When did you last start a dance at dinnertime with your left coattail in the cocktail and finish it with your right lapel in the soup?

Well, old man Hall and his gentle frau did, and we are now survivors of the voyage of the Black Queen. That would be the *Queen Mary*, really the pride of the British far-flung system of the seas...

In fact, if Mr. Rosy Ryan, boss of the Minneapolis Millers, can get some pitching like the *Queen Mary* delivered, he'll be all set.

There were two broken wrists, 90 broken dishes. I had trouble pushing my chair back and discovered why: It sensibly had been lassoed to the dining room deck. The swimming pool looked like Lake Michigan on a cranky day. You could negotiate the dance floor adroitly only if you had a ski tow for one direction and a toboggan for the other.

Aside from Neptune's indigestion, however, things were lovely.

Despite his many interests and avocations, Halsey remained most at home in a sports press box seated directly behind either a microphone or a typewriter. Like others, he had his opinions with regard to the changing nature of the world of sports, although he confined his on-air or in-print viewpoints to what took place on, not off, the field of play.

In 1971, however, Jim Meusey of the *St. Louis Park Sun* got Halsey to open up on a variety of topics concerning baseball at that time.

"To Halsey," Meusey wrote, "baseball, football, and basketball are still sports and not business as some proclaim.

"He dismisses the attempt by United States senators to eliminate baseball's exemption from anti-trust status as the efforts of a 'few disgruntled sourpusses.'

"He feels baseball player Curt Flood's suit challenging the reserve clause which binds him to a specific team for life is absurd. 'Criminy, the man is making $90,000 a year. How can he present himself as a slave or serf of the owners?' Halsey asks.

"Halsey admits dissatisfaction with the new vogue among pro athletes of writing 'tell all' books such as the one written by ex-pitcher Jim Bouton.

" 'I must admit I enjoyed the book,' Halsey said, 'but I still don't think he should have written about the players' private lives. It seems today that if anything is an exposé, it's going to sell a lot of books, even if it infringes on privacy.'

"According to Halsey, fans should read about a player's adventures on the field and not about his nocturnal wanderings."

Sue Kennedy adds that her dad didn't side with either the players or the owners in conflicts between labor and management. He agonized over a players' strike that delayed the opening of the 1972 season, and suffered again when a management lockout shut down spring training for a brief period in 1976.

Sue said that perhaps it was fortunate Halsey was no longer around to witness the 50-day strike in 1981 that wiped out a third of the season. "If he hadn't been cremated, he would have been spinning in his grave over that one," she adds. "Any kind of dissension he couldn't stand. He didn't care who was right or wrong; he just didn't like anything that interfered with the game.

"He would try not to pay any attention to it. It was just like when the sewer backed up and he got mad at Mother for going downstairs and discovering it. He felt like if he ignored the problem, maybe it would go away."

Accolades

Awards, honors, and tributes came to Halsey Hall in many ways during his lifetime.

An array of plaques and certificates adorned the walls of the Hall house on Alabama Avenue in recognition of his years of service in the field of sports. The lineup included an "Outstanding Achievement Award" from the Minneapolis Chamber of Commerce; an "Infectious Laughter Award" presented by the St. Louis Park Lions Club in November of 1971; a "Tomah Sportscaster Award" from WTMB Radio in Tomah, Wisconsin; plaques from the Minneapolis-St. Paul Minutemen and the Minnesota Broadcasters Association; a 1971 "Nice Guy Award" from the Twin Cities Chapter of the Baseball Writers Association of America (BBWAA); a "Sports World Man of the Year" award presented by the Minnesota Knights of Columbus in 1971; and the plaque he received from the National Sportscasters and Sportswriters Association when he was named Sportscaster of the Year in 1959.

In addition, there was a framed certificate proclaiming May 23, 1973 as Halsey Hall Day in the State of Minnesota. The honor, which commemorated his 75th birthday, was marked by a ceremony and party in the office of Governor Wendell Anderson.

Other special tributes Halsey received include the honor of being the grand marshal for the parade marking the 90th anniversary of the city of St. Louis Park in 1977, and being the guest of honor at the Spectators Club of Minneapolis in December of 1958. Stew MacPherson flew down from Winnipeg to preside as master of ceremonies at the latter event.

In August of 1975, Halsey was honored by the Minneapolis School Board for his contributions to high-school athletics. He was presented with a plaque prior to the Minneapolis City Conference football preview and then allowed to perform the ceremonial kickoff to start the event.

Some of the most meaningful encomiums, though, came not in the form of gold-plated trophies or plaques, but in the minds of those who knew Halsey.

"He was a wonderful man and had as good a sense of humor as anyone I ever met," said Gene Mauch, who played for both the Minneapolis Millers and St. Paul Saints and later managed the Minnesota Twins. "He was a beautiful person and a very fair reporter. He did everything a man could do in the media world."

"Halsey Hall was a truly fine gentleman and he always gave me a break," remembers Herb Hash, a pitcher for the Minneapolis Millers in the late 1930s.

Al Worthington, who pitched for both the Millers and the Twins, called Halsey "Mr. Midwest. I met him when I first came to the Millers in 1953, and he was always a favorite of mine."

A Miller teammate of Worthington's, Chuck Diering, remembered Halsey as being "very fair in his reporting when it came to writing about the abilities and personalities of the players. I always got along well with Halsey."

"He didn't have a mean bone in his whole body," added Marsh Ryman, the former athletic director at the University of Minnesota. "Halsey always wrote it the way he saw it. He never tried to develop an angle to make himself look good at someone else's expense."

"Of all the people who have been around in the media, he had the best hold and grasp of the game of anyone who's come along in my lifetime," says George Brophy, who served in various capacities with the

★★

"HOLY COW!"
You Betcha I'll Be There!

★★

TESTIMONIAL DINNER for

HALSEY HALL
at the RADISSON HOTEL

Cash Bar 5 P.M. — Mezzanine Floor   *Dinner Promptly at 6:30 P.M.*

WEDNESDAY, JULY 13th, 1966

★ TOASTMASTER — The One and Only Ray Scott.

★ SPEAKERS — Sports Celebrities and Dignitaries from Throughout the Country.

★ ENTERTAINMENT — An "All Star" Cast Headed by Boone and Erickson of WCCO.

★ SPECIAL FEATURES — Films, Photos and Tapes of Halsey Hall "In Action"!

★ ATTENDANCE — A Capacity Crowd Is Anticipated. (Women Are Welcome.)

★ RESERVATIONS — Special Tables for Purchasers of 10 or More Tickets.

(CLIP AND MAIL)

- -

YES! "I'll Be There If I Have to Borrow 'Holy Cows' Maxwell!"

SPORTS AND ATTRACTIONS COMMITTEE
MINNEAPOLIS CHAMBER OF COMMERCE
701 Second Avenue South, Minneapolis, Minn. 55402

Please send me .... tickets for the "Halsey Hall Testimonial Banquet", 6:30 P.M.,
Radisson Hotel Ballroom, Wednesday, July 13, 1966, at $10.00 each. My check, made
payable to the Minneapolis Chamber of Commerce, is enclosed.

NAME ....

FIRM ....

ADDRESS .... ZIP ....

More than 1,700 people turned out for a testimonial dinner honoring Halsey
in 1966.

The cover of the program for Halsey's 1966 testimonial.

Governor Wendell Anderson proclaimed Halsey Hall Day in Minnesota on May 23, 1973.

WCCO Radio's Howard Viken presides over Halsey Hall Appreciation Nite at the Suburban Sportsman's Club in February 1975.

Rev. William B.

For Halsey, the honors continued even after his death. Master of ceremonies Dave Mona and Sue Kennedy at the induction of Halsey Hall into the Minnesota Sports Hall of Fame November 15, 1989.

On May 4, 1985, Minnesota members of the Society for American Baseball Research (SABR) organized themselves as the Halsey Hall Chapter of SABR. The group's monthly newletter is named <u>The Holy Cow</u>.

THE "*HOLY COW*"

NEWSLETTER OF THE HALSEY HALL CHAPTER,
SOCIETY FOR AMERICAN BASEBALL RESEARCH

Millers and the Twins.

Ray Christensen, who shared a broadcast booth with Halsey for many years, said of his former partner, "Halsey was everybody's uncle."

Another erstwhile broadcast colleague, Ray Scott, added, "The things I remember most were his great zest for life and his fantastic sense of humor. Along with this, though, came a great sense of fair play. I never heard Halsey say anything ill of any other person.

"Isn't that a wonderful way to remember somebody?"

Possibly the greatest honor ever afforded Halsey was a 1966 testimonial dinner organized by Scott and Norm McGrew.

"The testimonial was Ray's idea," said McGrew. "He felt such an honor for Halsey was long overdue. As general manager of the Minneapolis Chamber of Commerce, I ran the Sports and Attractions Committee, a powerful group of more than 200 people interested in sports.

"We had no trouble getting these people involved. Everyone was enthusiastic about the idea and willing to help out for Halsey's sake."

Scott served as master of ceremonies for the dinner, which was held at the Hotel Radisson in downtown Minneapolis on Wednesday, July 13, 1966. The head-table luminaries included many local personalities— Paul Giel, Moose Goheen, Calvin Griffith, Dick Cullum, Frank Cleve, Charlie Johnson, Harmon Killebrew, Bernie Bierman, and Max Winter—as well as baseball executives Frank Lane, Bill Veeck, and Horace Stoneham, who were flown in to the banquet courtesy of Radisson owner Curt Carlson.

The dinner menu contained an assortment of entrees and appetizers, customized to suit the guest of honor, including Holy Cow Tossed Salad, Fresh Fruit Cup à la Sula, and Broiled Halsey Cut Sirloin Steak.

The highlight of the evening, according to McGrew, was the gift they came up with for Halsey. "Normally with this type of an affair," McGrew explained, "we'd give the guest a gold watch or something of that nature. We wanted to do more than that for Halsey.

"Bill Boyer, who owned the Ford dealership, was president of the Chamber at that time and told us he'd give us a deal on a car. With the override we had on the tickets we sold for the dinner and some extra money others chipped in, we had enough to buy a brand-new Ford Galaxie.

"I still remember the look on Halsey's face when we presented him a gold ignition key for the car. I don't think he ever got over that.

"The entire evening was perfect. If Ray and I were to do it over, the only thing we would have done different was gotten a bigger room for the event."

The Radisson's North Star Room was bursting that evening as more than seventeen hundred people— 1,706 to be exact—showed up to honor Halsey. It was the largest turnout ever in the state at that time for a testimonial dinner.

In his address, Bill Veeck, the former owner of the hapless St. Louis Browns, commented on the size of the aggregation. "To think that Halsey could outdraw the Browns," said Veeck. "With this kind of crowd, we would have played a doubleheader."

Bernie Bierman added, "I don't have to say what a heck of a guy Halsey is. It's obvious by the number of people who turned out for this tonight."

While most of the speakers talked of Halsey's long association with such sports as baseball, football, and basketball, Minnesota Vikings' owner Max Winter brought up another. "Everyone forgot to mention the sport Halsey really excelled at—pool.

"When I was a student at Hamline University, I often sat through my classes on an empty stomach. That's because I lost my lunch money to Halsey when we stopped off at the pool hall. He was quite a hustler."

Charlie Johnson, Halsey's former boss at the *Minneapolis Star*, capped his commentary with, "I salute you as a buddy who has made life so enjoyable for all of us."

In addition to the remarks and remembrances of those present, messages were read from a pair of men who were unable to attend—American League president Joe Cronin and United States Vice President Hubert Humphrey.

Finally, after two hours of plaudits, it was Halsey's turn to step to the microphone. And in inimitable Hall style he moved the audience from laughter to tears, sometimes simultaneously, as he ran the gamut from humorous to serious.

After opening with the statement, "I've been awfully nervous about this night for about two months...ever since I suggested it," Halsey began reading from a prepared text.

"You people aren't gathered here to honor an *ordinary* sportswriter, but one of the most *outstanding*...

"Holy Cow!" he then exclaimed, throwing down the manuscript. "This is the wrong speech!"

After rambling on with sports stories and humorous references to those who had preceded him on the dais, Halsey concluded his talk. "I wish I had some personal stationery so I could write each and every one of you to thank you for this tribute.

"My watermark would be a genuine tear of gratitude."

Halsey kicks off the 1975 City Conference football preview at Parade Stadium. Don Bevis, acting superintendent for the Minneapolis Public Schools, is his holder.

The Autumn Years

Although he left the Minnesota Twins broadcast crew following the 1972 season, Halsey remained a frequent visitor to Metropolitan Stadium. As the "Ambassador for Baseball," he presided over various pre-game ceremonies, such as those held on Opening Day, and also made guest appearances in the broadcast booths during selected home games.

Whether or not he had an official function, however, Halsey normally showed up for the games and found a spot in the Met Stadium press box, where he could chat with his former comrades. Each year, Twins' owner Calvin Griffith presented him with a pass that could be used not only at the Met, but at any American League ball park.

Semi-retirement left Halsey with more time for the simple pleasures he loved, such as watching soap operas or spending time with his family. Sula and he continued to travel, attending spring training with the Twins and serving as tour leaders on AAA cruises. And, ever the devotee of amusement parks, Halsey took his granddaughters to Walt Disney World in Orlando, Florida in 1974.

Unfortunately, 1974 was also the year that Halsey began to be plagued with a series of physical ailments. Cataract surgery in January left him with a patch over his right eye for several weeks. He recovered quickly and even used the eyepatch as part of his costume when he dressed up for a Mardi Gras party during a Caribbean cruise in early March.

The eye problems, however, affected his nighttime vision and, from that point on, he did little driving in the evening. His daughter had to drive him to Met

Stadium for night games, and he would catch a lift home from one of his friends.

After getting home from one such game in late May of 1974, around the time of his 76th birthday, Halsey was undressing when he felt a pain in his chest. "I don't feel well," he said to Sula as he sat down on the edge of the bed. Within moments, however, the discomfort subsided and he went to sleep without giving it any more thought.

Two weeks later, on June 4, he was with his daughter when he began experiencing difficulty breathing. Sue called Dr. Harvey O'Phelan, one of the Twins' team physicians and a longtime family friend (Halsey had worked with O'Phelan's father, Jim, 50 years before at the *St. Paul Pioneer Press*), and then drove her dad to O'Phelan's office in downtown Minneapolis.

"It was a hair-raising ride downtown," recalls Sue. "Daddy was huffing and puffing—having a terrible time breathing. The problem, as it turned out, was with his heart."

According to O'Phelan, Halsey was in cardiac decompensation (experiencing heart failure) and had an arterial occlusion (blood clot) of the left leg, which was related to the decompensation.

"The blood clot came from the heart and traveled to the leg," O'Phelan explained, adding that the chest pain Halsey had felt two weeks before had probably been a minor heart attack. "Following the heart attack, he gradually went into cardiac decompensation. The problem finally manifested itself with the breathing difficulties he experienced on June 4."

O'Phelan immediately arranged for Halsey to be admitted to nearby St. Mary's Hospital. Although his condition stabilized quickly, Halsey remained in the hospital for almost 11 weeks. He also underwent an operation on June 15 to improve the blood circulation in his lower leg.

Visitors were restricted immediately following surgery, but plenty of friends eventually called on Halsey during his confinement. While he appreciated the company, he lamented the fact that he was unable to have a drink. Norm McGrew recalls how Bob Short (a Minneapolis hotel owner and political maverick as well as the absentee owner of the Texas Rangers) solved the problem. "Even though it was the middle of summer," said McGrew, "Short brought Halsey a Christmas tree as a present. The tree was loaded with decorations that were actually small bottles of liquor.

"By the time Halsey left the hospital, he had drank that tree dry."

His stay in the hospital caused Halsey to miss a couple of events at which he dearly would have loved to have been present. One was his granddaughter Cindy's high-school graduation. The other—on Sunday, August 11—was Harmon Killebrew Day at Met Stadium when the Twins paid homage to their greatest slugger.

Under normal circumstances, Halsey would have been master of ceremonies for the Killebrew Day festivities; in his absence Bob Fowler of the *Minneapolis Star* presided.

Halsey was released from St. Mary's Hospital on August 16, 1974, although he was readmitted for cardiac rehabilitation six days later and remained until the 30th of August.

Halsey felt fit when he finally checked out of the hospital, but this would not be the end of his ailments. The following winter he began experiencing numbness in his left foot caused by two small ulcers in his heel, a residual effect of the occlusion from the year before.

On March 2, 1975 he was back in the hospital, prompting him to wryly quip that he felt like he "owned a wing of St. Mary's." A bypass operation was performed and Halsey remained hospitalized for approximately four weeks.

While the length of Halsey's stay was less than half that of the previous year, it was a more difficult confinement according to his daughter. "The surgery left him flat on his back," said Sue. "Mother and I were down there every day watching soap operas with him from 10:30 in the morning to three o'clock in the afternoon.

"Those soaps got all three of us through this period."

Halsey never regained full use of his foot. He was issued a cane, although his daughter reports that his vanity sometimes made him reluctant to use it.

"He didn't want people to think he was an invalid," she said. When he was hosting ceremonies before a Twins game, he'd leave the cane in the dugout and hobble out to home plate without it.

"He also had to take pills every day, and he even made a fuss about this. Finally, one of the doctors asked him, 'Halsey, would you rather take a few pills or have your foot cut off?'

"That was the end of that argument."

The 1975 health problems caused Halsey to miss spring training with the Twins for the first time ever; he was back on his feet, however, in time for a special function on May 4.

Following the 1974 season, Killebrew had left the Twins and signed a contract with the Kansas City Royals for what would be his final season as a player. On the Royals' first 1975 visit of the season to Met Stadium, the Twins honored Killebrew by retiring his number 3, which he had worn during his years with the team. Killebrew was back in Minnesota, at least for the time being, and Halsey was back behind the microphone for the pre-game ceremonies at home plate.

On Friday, January 30, 1976, Halsey was scheduled to take part in a testimonial dinner and "roast" of Senator Hubert Humphrey. Sponsored by the Minnesota Press Club, the event was held at the Radisson Hotel in downtown Minneapolis. Other roasters on the program included Minnesota Vikings defensive tackle Alan Page; Governor Wendell Anderson; David Roe, head of the Minnesota AFL-CIO; Senator Walter Mondale; economist Walter Heller; satirist Dudley Riggs; former Minnesota Governor Karl Rolvaag; Charles W. Bailey, editor of the *Minneapolis Tribune*; Republican National committeeman (and future Senator) Rudy Boschwitz; federal judge Miles Lord; and Bob DeHaven of WCCO Radio, the master of ceremonies.

The evening was to be special, not just for Halsey, but for Sula as well because this would be the first time she would be allowed to join her husband at the head table for such an event. In the past, head tables had been reserved only for those taking part in the program. (Even at the 1966 testimonial dinner for Halsey, Sula sat at a separate table with other family members.)

At the Humphrey affair, however, spouses were welcome at the head table. For weeks Sula looked forward to the opportunity to finally sit with Halsey at a banquet. The morning of the event, her daughter got her up at seven o'clock and took her to the beauty shop.

That evening, Sue drove her parents downtown and dropped them off at the Radisson. Following a private cocktail party in the Minnesota Press Club, one floor above the room in which the dinner would be held, the head table guests descended a back stairway and entered the banquet hall.

The 700 people in attendance applauded as the entourage made its way in a formal procession to the head table, which was on a raised platform. A set of steps had been placed at the end of the platform to allow access to the dais. The small stairway, however, had no bannister, and the Halls were forced to hang onto to one another for support.

As they made their way up the steps, Halsey lost his balance and fell backward, taking Sula with him. Halsey's fall was broken by the Rolvaags behind him. Sula, however, was not as fortunate; she cracked her head on the floor.

Governor Anderson immediately summoned his chauffeur and had him take Sula, along with Halsey, to General Hospital a few blocks away. After being examined, Sula was released and the Halls were transported home in the governor's limousine.

Before they left the hospital, Halsey called his daughter and told her of the accident. "I met them at their house and decided to spend the night," she said. "Mother said she had a headache but, beyond that, she appeared to be all right, so Daddy went to bed.

"Around one or two o'clock, Mother started hallucinating. She said she saw her sister Katie, who was dead. At this point, her headache disappeared. When she started vomiting a couple hours later, I called the hospital and was told to get her down there right away. I woke up Daddy and we got Mother in the car. By this time, she was catatonic.

"When we got to the hospital, they discovered she had a blood clot on her brain and operated immediately.

"Before we had left their house for the dinner the night before, I had taken the prettiest picture of them. Mother was so proud of her new hairdo. A few hours later, her hair was down and a mess. By the next morning, her hair was completely gone."

Sue also recalls that when her mother woke up following the surgery, her first words were spoken in German. "She started speaking English again right away. One thing she never recovered, though, was her emotions.

"The accident had completely robbed her of any emotion."

After two weeks in General Hospital, Sula was transferred to Methodist Hospital in St. Louis Park; she was released shortly after and returned home with Halsey.

"When she first got home, she was able to cook and do housework," said Sue, "but her condition deteriorated.

"She got more sedentary and became forgetful. Once, after Daddy had gone to bed, she boiled a pan of water and left it on the stove. The next day I came over and found the pan welded to the electric burner.

"Mother got worse and worse. A couple of times she made fires in the fireplace and let the logs roll out onto the rug. I was afraid she was going to burn the house down. It was obvious something had to be done."

In March of 1977, Sue reluctantly put her mother in the Edina Care Center on 62nd Street and Xerxes Avenue in Edina, Minnesota. "I did it while Daddy was in Florida for spring training with the Twins," said Sue. "He agreed with the decision to put her in a nursing home, but we both knew it would be more difficult if he were present.

"Mother would have prevailed upon him to let her stay at home and he probably would have given in. If he had been there, I don't think I ever would have gotten her in the care center."

The Halls filed a $400,000 lawsuit against the Radisson Hotel Corporation as a result of the accident. The suit asked for $300,000 for Sula's injuries, pain, and suffering and $100,000 for Halsey for loss of his wife's "care, comfort, and society."

The complaint alleged that the hotel "breached its warranty to provide safe premises" and also claimed that the stairs leading up to the dais were "defective and dangerous" and that there was negligence on the part of the hotel employees.

The suit was eventually settled, out of court, for approximately $60,000.

Sula was to outlive her husband (she died March 10, 1979, 14 months after Halsey). However, said Sue, "For all practical purposes, my mother died on January 30, 1976 when she hit her head on the floor at the Radisson Hotel.

"I don't mean to be flip, but to this day when people ask who died first—my mother or my dad—I have trouble answering."

Sue said that her mother never did adjust to life in a nursing home, nor did Halsey ever adjust to life without Sula. "He'd visit her regularly at the care center, but it wasn't the same. He missed her terribly."

It wasn't her father's nature to complain, however. "He was always like that—never showing his emotions except for happiness. With Mother gone, though, there wasn't much happiness. Even so, he tried to cover his sadness.

"No matter what, he always put up a brave front."

December 30, 1977

December 30, 1977 began like most other days for Halsey Hall. He reached out his front door to pick up the Friday morning edition of the *Minneapolis Tribune* from the steps and then scanned the front page of the newspaper.

"Carter begins his trip proclaiming friendship" read the headline of the lead story regarding President Jimmy Carter's arrival in Warsaw to begin a six-nation European tour. Another article detailed the foiled efforts of a pair of Minneapolis police officers who had traveled to New York to help Minnesota teenagers escape the clutches of prostitution on Times Square. At the bottom of the page was a brief weather forecast calling for cloudy skies with a chance of snow flurries in the evening.

Tucked well inside the front section was a small item about Polish communist party chief Edward Gierek sending greetings to Minnesota Senator Hubert Humphrey, who was suffering from inoperable cancer.

A *Tribune* special section titled "A look back at 1977" summarized some of the year's major stories: the death of Elvis Presley; the Mideast peace initiative of Egyptian president Anwar Sadat; the June murder of 83-year-old heiress Elisabeth Congdon in her Duluth mansion; the state legislature's passage of a bill authorizing a new sports stadium for the Twin Cities; and the return of the Little Brown Jug to Minnesota possession for the first time in ten years, as the Gopher football team shocked the top-ranked Michigan Wolverines with a 16-0 victory in October (an event which no doubt pleased Halsey).

The main story in the sports section was of the Minnesota Vikings' upcoming game with the Dallas Cowboys for the National Football Conference championship and a berth in the Super Bowl. One of the Vikings, defensive end Jim Marshall, was celebrating his 40th birthday on this day, it was reported in Sid Hartman's column.

Later in the morning, satisfied that he was sufficiently apprised on world affairs, Halsey got into his car and drove the short distance to the King's Inn on Excelsior Boulevard. Friday was Clam Chowder day at the King's Inn, and Halsey maintained his weekly ritual of picking up a bowl to go, then getting home by noon in time to eat lunch while watching his favorite soap opera, "All My Children."

In between the rest of his soap operas that afternoon, Halsey spent time studying a copy of the Minnesota Driving Manual. Because of the difficulty he had with walking since his bypass operation two years earlier, Halsey's daughter had finally convinced him to apply to the state for a handicapped-parking permit. The state granted his request, but along with the permit came a notice that Halsey would be required to pass a written and driving test to maintain his license.

The test was scheduled for the second week of 1978; Sue Kennedy was not optimistic over her father's chances of passing the test. "He did very little driving at that time," she said. "He only took the car out during the day and never went on the highway. He drove only to familiar places like the grocery store or the King's Inn or to see Mother at the nursing home.

"But having a car meant independence for Daddy, and I was afraid of what would happen to him if he were no longer allowed to drive."

Sue kept in daily contact with Halsey. Being aware

of her dad's viewing habits, she timed her phone calls so as not to interfere with his favorite television shows. On Friday nights, she normally squeezed in a call between "Quincy" and "The Rockford Files."

On this Friday, however, a particularly funny rerun of "The Carol Burnett Show" prompted an earlier-than-usual phone call. Knowing that her dad, a loyal Burnett fan, would also have been watching, Sue called at the conclusion of the show at 6:30 so the two could share a laugh.

At the end of the conversation with his daughter, Halsey walked into the kitchen and pulled his TV dinner out of the oven. After placing the dinner on the counter to cool, he reached for a bottle of Scotch his granddaughter Cindy had given him for Christmas and prepared to pour a drink.

He was unscrewing the cap when the heart attack struck. The coroner later said he was probably dead before he hit the floor.

Since she had just talked to her father, Sue didn't call back at the usual time. She wouldn't have received an answer if she had.

Overnight, the predicted flurries materialized into much more, and by Saturday morning several inches of snow covered the ground. Sue walked to an appointment at a beauty shop down the street from her home and, upon returning at 10:45, called her dad.

Although she found it strange that he didn't answer, Sue decided to wait a few minutes before panicking. When another call 20 minutes later also went unanswered, however, her concern turned to alarm.

She called the Harrisons, who lived across the street from Halsey, and asked them to check on her dad. Pat Harrison called right back to report that no tire tracks or footprints were visible in the fresh snow around the house or garage. It was apparent that Halsey had not gone out.

Harrison then grabbed a set of keys to the Hall house and headed back across the street. He let himself in through the back door and immediately saw Halsey sprawled on the floor, the bottle of Scotch clutched tightly in his arms.

He called Sue, but found himself having difficulty conveying the news.

"There's been an accident," Pat told her.

"Well, did you call an ambulance?" asked Sue.

"It's too late for that," came the reply.

Sue didn't comprehend the meaning of Harrison's last statement and asked her husband and daughter Cindy to drive over and investigate.

Twenty minutes later Bill phoned Sue to confirm what she suspected but didn't want to believe.

Bill had also called the police, who notified the press, and news of Halsey's death spread quickly. Sue called the Edina Care Center, where her mother was a resident, and asked them to turn off all the radios. "I didn't want her finding out that way," Sue explained. Ruth Hirshfield, Sue's longtime friend, volunteered to go to the nursing home and tell Sula what had happened.

Meanwhile, the news of Halsey's death was dominating the programming on WCCO Radio, where Halsey had worked for so many years. Several former colleagues were contacted and put on the air to relate their memories of him.

Another colleague and one of Halsey's closest friends, Ray Scott, was in Palo Alto, California announcing the Shrine East-West football game when he heard about Halsey from Joe Boyle of WTCN-TV, the station carrying the game in the Twin Cities. Scott immediately passed the news on to the national television audience. "Halsey had many friends and followers across the country," said Scott.

The cause of death was listed as "Cardiac arrest due to severe coronary sclerosis." The death certificate, signed by Dr. Andrew Shea, also mentioned the heart problems Halsey had experienced three years before.

By Saturday evening, Sue and Bill Kennedy were ready to discuss the funeral arrangements. "Daddy hadn't wanted a funeral of any type," said Sue, "but Bill convinced me that we should at least have a small service."

Private services were held for Halsey on Monday, January 2 at the Werness Brothers Funeral Chapel in south Minneapolis. In addition to the family, a few of Sue's friends were present, along with some of Halsey's closest friends, including Tony Oliva and Rod Carew of the Twins, Herb Carneal, Norm McGrew, Harvey O'Phelan, and Ray Scott.

A picture of Halsey rested on top of the closed casket. And as a tribute to Halsey's long association with University of Minnesota athletics, the organist slipped in a dirge-like version of the Minnesota Rouser. "At that point," recalled Scott, "there wasn't a dry eye in the house."

Halsey was cremated at Lakewood Cemetery and his remains interred at Fort Snelling National Cemetery.

His will, which he had drafted in 1961, was simple and straightforward. Halsey stipulated that all his belongings be left to his wife, Sula Bornman Hall, or, in the event that she had preceded him in death, to his daughter, Suzanne Eugenia Hall Kennedy.

Halsey concluded his will with this paragraph: *"I know full well that my life has been happier because of my Sula and Suzanne and may God's blessing be on them and on William Charles Kennedy and my adored grandchildren, William Halsey Kennedy, Kathryn Sula Kennedy, Cynthia Eugenia Kennedy."*

R.I.P.

194

Gone But Not Forgotten

"I am bereft," wrote Jean Carlson of Pine City, Minnesota in a letter to the *Minneapolis Star* editorial page following the death of Halsey Hall. "I shall miss his marvelous laugh, his love of mundane things, like onions and cigars, his ready wit and his true caring about fans and players alike," continued Carlson, who echoed the sentiments of fans throughout the region with the last line of her letter: "Holy Cow! I have lost a friend."

The void left by the passing of Halsey became particularly noticeable when the 1978 baseball season opened. The "Welcome Home Luncheon" for the Twins was the first ever that did not have Halsey at the head table. "It just doesn't seem right," said Herb Carneal, Halsey's longtime broadcast partner.

Metropolitan Stadium employees became acutely aware of Halsey's absence early in the season when a half-eaten platter of green onions was left behind in the press room after a pre-game meal. "Before, there were never any onions left," said Vi Turner of the stadium's culinary staff. "Halsey saw to that."

One of the dining areas at the Met, the Minnesota Room, was renamed the Halsey Hall Room by the Twins. This would be a shortlived honor, however, since Met Stadium was in its final years. Plans were already underway to build a new sports stadium in the Twin Cities. By the end of 1978, it was decided that the new stadium would be a domed facility in downtown Minneapolis.

Many of Halsey's friends, led by Dick Cullum, lobbied the Metropolitan Sports Facilities Commission to name the stadium after Halsey. In the end, however, the commission stuck to its original decision to name it after Hubert Humphrey (who had died on Friday, January 13, 1978, exactly a fortnight following the death of Halsey).

In May of 1985, a group of baseball researchers and fans—all members of the Society for American Baseball Research (SABR)—voted to organize themselves into a local chapter of SABR. They then tackled the question of what to call themselves. Various options were discussed, but none seemed right until John DiMeglio, one of the charter members of the group, said, "Let's name it after Halsey." With that, the Halsey Hall Chapter of the Society for American Baseball Research was born. The group publishes a monthly newsletter appropriately named *The Holy Cow*.

Another posthumous honor came to Halsey on Wednesday, November 15, 1989 when he was inducted into the Minnesota Sports Hall of Fame. Sue Kennedy was present to accept her father's Hall of Fame plaque, which now hangs with those of other enshrinees at the Humphrey Metrodome. Dave Mona, who served as master of ceremonies for the induction luncheon at the Minneapolis Athletic Club, said, "When I first became aware that the Minnesota Sports Hall of Fame existed, I automatically assumed that Halsey Hall was a member.

"Now he finally is."

Great interest in Halsey remains even years after his death. When she took to the speaker's circuit with her "Life With Father—Halsey, That Is" presentation, Sue Kennedy found herself in greater demand than she ever anticipated.

Newspaper writers, not just in the Twin Cities but throughout the region, continue to find Halsey a rich and inexhaustible source of material for their columns.

In 1984, Nick Coleman of the *Minneapolis Star and Tribune* wrote, "Halsey Hall was a legend who will live forever in the consciousness of Minnesota."

Two years later, John Egan, a columnist for the *Argus Leader* of Sioux Falls, South Dakota, covered the Twins' Silver Anniversary Banquet. Egan wrapped up his column with this paragraph:

"Through it all, one thing is hauntingly missing—the sweet sounds of Halsey telling us what is happening."

Appendix

Halsey Hall stories that appeared in "Best Sports Stories" publications (reprinted with the permission of the *Minneapolis Star and Tribune*):

1929

Game One of the 1929 World Series. Philadelphia Athletics' manager Connie Mack shocks the baseball world by selecting 35-year-old Howard Ehmke to pitch the series opener at Wrigley Field in Chicago. Ehmke, however, responds with a four-hitter to beat Joe McCarthy's Cubs, 3-1, and in the process strikes out 13 Chicago batters to set a new World Series record.

(Attendance at this game was 50,740, far in excess of Wrigley Field's usual capacity. The additional crowd was accommodated by extra bleachers that were built on the street behind the outfield fences.)

Chicago, Oct. 8—It is reported that Abraham Lincoln, once the manager of the United States, was told that General Grant had been drinking and Abraham Lincoln said, "Find out what he drinks and give it to the rest of my generals."

Wherefore, we find today the unusual situation in which Howard Ehmke, a pitcher who has been disciplined by Connie Mack for being a trouble maker and disturber and anything but a right sort of liver, is the hero of an opening World Series game. It is natural to suppose, therefore, that Mr. Mack now will insist all his pitchers become trouble makers and castoffs and then how will you stop the Athletics?

He is one up now, one up by usage of an old castoff and troublemaker and with Grove, Earnshaw and Walberg as fresh as the new landlord, ready to shoot at the Cubs who have used Root and Bush in a losing cause and who will pitch Pat Malone today.

Listen, here is Howard Ehmke.

A castoff, a putrid castoff of two big league teams, standing six feet, three inches tall, gangling, angular, waving in pitching motion as the cornstalks of an Iowa field. Here is Howard Ehmke, not much meat on his bones, not very wide, not very strong, but 665 feet broad across the heart and fathoms deep in that same organ, that organ of bravery that stood by him out there in a warm October sun and stood Chicago's Cubs on their heads.

The Cubs were Cublets yesterday as Ehmke slow-curved them across to a 3 to 1 victory in as dramatic a World Series opener as any year ever saw. Fifty-one thousand persons came to cheer the Cubs, 51,000 persons dwindled to 25,000 midway in the game, for the other 25,000 were cheering Ehmke, and, when tall Howard shuffled his lazy way to bat in the ninth inning, 51,000 fans cheered him to the echo. He had not only beaten the Cubs, he had won the admiration of the Chicago rooters.

They said the Cubs could hit fast ball pitchers, but what did they say about the slow ones? Surely, no pitcher ever threw a tantalizing slow ball such as Howard Ehmke threw yesterday and as the sun disappeared behind the left field stands, so disappeared the hitting hopes of the Cublets.

Those poisonous batsmen had their outbreak once

or twice. Bless you, yes, they had to break out once in a while, but they represented the lightest attack of batting measles that anybody ever saw. Ehmke had a great stock in trade. It consisted of a slow curve, a slower curve and a slowest curve and there were the men of McCarthy swinging for the dear old backbreak, swinging from their ankles and twisting their jaws all out of shape as they grunted at the passing ball. Ehmke threw a fast one, yes. We believe he threw about three in the whole game and, when he powdered them in there, they were missed just like the slow ones. The Cubs played no favorites.

It's easy to hit a slow ball if you're used to it, but the National League should have passed a ruling that pitchers facing the Cubs in the closing stages of the campaign must throw slow balls. That is the greatest fallacy in baseball, the idea of trying to throw them by somebody and Mr. Ehmke has added a new patent to his line. You know Howard is independently wealthy from something or other that he has patented in Detroit and now is roosting high and dry on the proceeds of his slow ball patent. Mr. Ehmke probably will go along patenting things until he has patented himself to a rich and ripe old age and if they are not starting now to exact a monument to him in Philadelphia, there is something the matter with Phil's civic pride.

The best hope for the Cubs today was to call upon some of the Chicago gunmen. Some of the gunmen might have shown them how to do a little exploding, but they couldn't have dented that iron heart that belonged to Howard Ehmke. Once or twice he wavered and at the finish of the game Connie Mack had Grove, then Earnshaw, then Walberg warming up in the bullpen along the right field stands.

As Ehmke went slow speed ahead to break Ed

Walsh's strikeout record of 12 against the Cubs in
1906, he played no favorites. He fanned Cuyler twice
and Hornsby twice and twice he got Hornsby, Wilson
and Cuyler in a row. Again he fanned McMillan, English, Hornsby and Wilson in a row and he also struck
out two pinch hitters. The only pinch in the afternoon
belonged to these hitters, we can tell you that, and he
saved his record breaking strikeout of the afternoon
for Slug Tolson, the last batter, with runners on first
and third and the count three and two.

Drama? Say, this old ball game was choking with it.
Charley Root, pitching for the Cubs, was just as good
as Ehmke, barring the strikeout touch, and for six
innings Ehmke's slow curve and Root's sharp breaking
wrinkle ball were masters of the day. It was a sight to
see and the crowd was in a frenzy as one batter after
another bit the dust and one fielder after another came
up with a sensational play.

There was Jimmy Dykes diving full length to his left
to come up with a Stephenson liner, there was Al
Simmons picking a foul off the left field bleacher wall
with one hand, and there was Hack Wilson throwing
his pianoesque frame headlong into the turf to rob
Simmons of a slow line hit.

And so it went until the seventh inning when Jimmy
Foxx overpowered the ball and sent it into the deepest
corner of the center field bleachers. That sent the
Macks wild on the bench and that made it necessary
for the Cubs to use some pinch hitters as Ehmke got
himself into trouble in the seventh. Here it is:

Cuyler sent one down to short that Boley couldn't
handle and Stephenson sent one over third for a single.
The fans woke up and they stayed awake when Grimm
advanced the runners with a beautiful sacrifice. Zach
Taylor hadn't been hitting, so McCarthy sent in Cliff

Heathcote, a lefthanded batsman and Heathcote lifted a short fly just back of Boley's position. It was interesting then to see the perfect formation that the Macks went into, just like a football team going through its shift. Boley ran away from short and backed up third while Dykes stood on the base. Simmons came running into short left for the fly. Ehmke and Foxx went to Cochrane's assistance at the plate. Simmons caught the ball and fired it home and there wasn't a chance for Cuyler to score.

Hartnett batted for Root and Ehmke struck him out and Bush and Gonzalez became the Chicago battery. Things were peaceful in the eighth but the Macks went ahead to sew it up in the ninth and give Woody English, at short, a good running start toward being the goat.

Cochrane singled and Simmons hit a double play ball to English that he booted. Foxx hit one in the same spot and English, taking the ball and getting set, popped it out of his bare hand. It looked like a good choke play. This filled the base and two came home on Bing Miller's sounding single over Bush's head and out into centerfield, but Long Guy put on the brakes and it is well he did.

Well, the Cubs had to bat, although it didn't seem as if there would be much use in their going through the motions. Wilson tore loose a terrific liner that Ehmke knocked down to get his man at first. Big Howard then collapsed. After writhing on the ground for a minute or so he got up, threw a practice pitch or two and was ready to go.

So were the Cubs. Cuyler hit a slow bounder to Dykes and that young man, with a fine show of strong arm and not much sense of distance, cut loose a lurid heave past Foxx that gave Cuyler two bases.

Stephenson singed a single to center, scoring Cuyler, and Grimm dropped one into right, with all hands cheering and Eddie Collins rushing out for the big conference with Cochrane and Ehmke. Howard stayed in, however, and Blair, batting for Gonzalez, forced Grimm at second. And then came Tolson to hit for Bush and the final strikeout of the day.

You might have expected some moaning as those disgruntled Cublet followers took their way out of the stands, but here was no moaning—just admiration for Mr. Ehmke and his job. And Mr. Ehmke can have his job, too, thought Connie Mack as he was rolled downtown in an automobile seated between two elderly women and an elderly man with a look on his face as of a man who has a sour apple in his mouth. We wonder what it takes to make Connie smile.

1946

In 1946, the Brooklyn Dodgers, managed by Leo Durocher, and St. Louis Cardinals, behind Eddie Dyer, finished the regular season in a first-place tie with 96-58 records. For the first time in major-league history, a playoff was needed to determine the league champion.

The Cardinals took the first game of a best-of-three series; another victory would give them their fourth National League pennant in five years and a berth in the World Series against the Boston Red Sox. Here is Halsey's report on the second playoff game, held at Ebbets Field in Brooklyn:

Brooklyn, N. Y., October 3—Lippy Leo Durocher threw the book at the Cardinals yesterday and the Cardinals turned the pages.

Right-hander Murry Dickson, with a deep freeze system for a heart and a bushmaster's whip for an arm, twirled the men of Missouri to victory, 8-4, for two straight over Brooklyn in the first playoff series in major league history.

And so the National League toga is edged in cardinal instead of the blue and white of the Bums, and that blue and white was black and blue this sunny Thursday.

How did the wild-eyed Dodger rooters take it? Well, with cheers and jeers, sighs, groans, sarcasm, and an odd mixture of philosophy. It was "Atta boy, Joe," to Hatten at the start. It was "That's it, Joe. We'll get you out of it" in the first flurry of Cardinal power.

But the storm grew into a tornado that blew Ebbets Field apart, leaving only downcast Dodger debris strewn around the premises.

Then it was "Ya bum, ya," and, when Kurowski drove out a bases-filled single in the Cardinal eighth, somebody yelled "Everybody home. C'mon, everybody, leave the park." From a hundred ramps streamed hundreds of the crowd of 31,437, turning their backs on a cruel 1946.

There were cheers for Murry Dickson midway in the game whenever he came to bat. In fact, these sincerely insane Bum supporters do give visiting players a hand. It is as if they palmed a brick while casting a bouquet.

Then came the ninth and the beating away of Dickson by the suddenly surging wave of Brooklyn power. Tired by his batting and running, falling heir to the human frailty of easing up, Dickson didn't blow—he exploded.

And where the Dodgers had made no hits from the first inning and had hit only three balls to the outfield in eight heart-searing frames of futility, they routed Dickson.

There were 900 individual cheer leaders in the crowd then. One leather-lunged female directed her whole section of the stands. At irregular spaces along the second-deck rail, well-dressed gentlemen removed their hats and coats and went into cheer-leading action.

Augie Galan doubled, Ed Stevens tripled, Carl Furillo singled, Pee Wee Reese walked, Bruce Edwards singled.

Harry Brecheen, "The Cat," came to the mound. Cookie Lavagetto batted for Harry Taylor, the sixth Dodger twirler, and walked.

Then, with the outfield reaches freckled with cast-off programs, the shadows falling long and bedlam in complete control, the spidery Brecheen went to work. He slipped a third strike past Eddie Stanky. Howie Schultz came up to hit for left fielder Whitman and got the count up to 3-2.

He swung wildly at the next one, and the Cards made for the World Series while the crowd made for the Cards.

Brecheen's cap was torn off as catcher Clyde Kluttz ran out to give him the victory ball. Manager Eddie Dyer took off under full steam to greet his pitcher and the whole flock of incoming Cardinals was engulfed in a downpouring of the Brooklynites. Six policemen bulled into the melee, which looked dangerous but which was only Dodger exuberance. Brecheen and also Kluttz left sans caps and with hair rumpled every which way.

So endeth a dramatic series, worthy to be remembered as the only one of its kind for the pennant. The tension held hard through the stands until the fifth, when St. Louis exercised its hickory mastery and Leo Durocher third- and fourth-guessed himself out of the ball game.

Singles by Galan and Stevens with a walk to Dixie Walker had given Joe Hatten a 1-0 lead in the first, but it lasted only until the Cardinal breezes of the second could blow around Ebbets Field.

Erv Dusak, who earlier in the year had hit a clutch home run for the Cards, drove a hearty triple to left center and scored on Marty Marion's fly. There were two out, but Clyde Kluttz singled to right, and right here Eddie Dyer's strategy in pitching Dickson for his hitting ability against southpaws bore fruit. The willowy right hander kissed one to the gate in deep right center and it was another triple and two runs.

The real blowoff was the fifth, and in typical Ebbets Field fashion, it happened with two down. Stan Musial scorched a screaming double to right, and Durocher ordered Kurowski passed for Slaughter, who only led the National League in runs batted in. Mr. Slaughter promptly tripled off the right field wall and when Dusak singled him home, Hank Behrman went to the mound to get the side out.

Well, that was it. Vic Lombardi, Kirby Higbe, Rube Melton and Harry Taylor followed Behrman either in relief or pinch-hitting order.

There was a Card tally in the seventh on walks to Kurowski and Slaughter, Dusak's sacrifice and Marion's perfect squeeze bent, which drew an out for him but got the run across.

In the eighth, strategy went topsy-turvy. Schoendienst singled and Moore doubled to the left-field corner, the ball bouncing from Dixie Walker's glove into the stands for a ground-rule hit. Then Musial was purposely passed for Kurowski, the guy they had purposely passed for Slaughter, and Whitey brought the blue chorus of boos to a fine crescendo with a two-run single into right field.

By this time you looked for Bum rooters' hearts among their shoelaces. But they were back in their mouths in that ninth inning, thereby setting some sort of record for heart elevation. As Durocher led each Dodger hurler from the mound, the crowd swallowed its downheartedness and gave vent to applause.

It was as if they were sending each mound warrior, who had hurled the Brooks into a pennant tie, down that last long trail with a "Well done, old man, see you next year."

1947

In 1947, the Brooklyn Dodgers were trying to win their first World Series. It was their fourth appearance in the Fall Classic, and their second against the New York Yankees.

Some would say the Dodgers had never been blessed with the best of luck in post-season struggles.

They fell to the Red Sox in 1916 with one of their losses coming at the hands of Boston's ace lefthander, Babe Ruth, who went the distance in a 14-inning thriller (still the longest game in Series history).

Four years later, it was the Cleveland Indians turn to beat up on the Brooks. In the fifth game, the Dodgers were victimized to a series of Series' firsts: a grand slam (by Elmer Smith); a home run by a pitcher (Jim Bagby); and a unassisted triple play (Bill Wambsganss performing the feat that has yet to be repeated in a World Series).

An even stranger loss haunted the Dodgers in 1941. They led the Yankees by a run with two out in the ninth inning of Game Four when Hugh Casey struck out Tommy Henrich to apparently end the game. But Brooklyn backstop Mickey Owen was unable to hang on to the pitch and, as the ball rolled away, Henrich sprinted safely to first. The Yankees made the most of the miscue as they turned it into a four-run rally to win the game and eventually the series.

In 1947, however, Brooklyn backers thought their luck might be changing as they watched the Dodgers pull out an incredible victory in Game Four to tie the series at two games apiece. Not only did the Dodgers trail by a run entering the last of the ninth of this game, they were without a hit against the Yankees' Floyd (Bill) Bevens. A pair of walks put runners at first and second with two out when Cookie Lavagetto, sent to the plate as a pinch hitter by manager Burt Shotton, stroked a two-run double off the right-field fence. On one pitch, Bevens had lost both his no-hitter and the game.

The Yankees won the next day to regain the lead in the series, but the Dodgers have an 8-5 lead in the sixth inning of Game Six. With two out, the Yankees have two runners aboard when Joe DiMaggio hits a long drive to left...

New York, October 5—Did you ever see boy reach for a star? And grasp it?

Seventy-four thousand and sixty-five fans saw it this afternoon at the colossal Yankee Stadium as the Bums of Brooklyn squared the most delirious World Series ever played, beating the Yankees, 8-6.

As a deep-throated roar rent the autumn air, Joe DiMaggio touched the fuse to a shot high and far toward left center. The only odds were on whether it was a home run, or a triple. There were two out, two were on and the Yankees trailed, 8-5.

Racing backward from a normal left-field position was Al Gionfriddo, sixth choice in the Burt Shotton grab bag of outfielders. Racing over from center came Carl Furillo with no chance at all except to help watch where that herculean blast would fall. And then Gionfriddo reached for that star.

Turning suddenly from his headlong middle-distance run, Gionfriddo reached up to pluck that ball. As he caught it, his hands were over the railing of the swinging gate which leads to the visitors' bullpen. He tumbled half over the gate as the charging Furillo virtually landed on his back.

Gionfriddo literally caught a home run out of the park and graybeards of the press, visiting heroes like Rogers Hornsby and others, are unwilling to say there ever has been a classmate to this catch, which wins valedictorian awards in any class of outfield defense.

They cheered Gionfriddo for five minutes of the three hours and 19 minutes (a new record) it took to play this melodrama.

He was first up next inning and grounded out peacefully. The crowd set up a new cheering symphony to his footsteps all the way from first base back to the Brooklyn dugout.

These Dodgers who never have learned to spell L-O-S-E must make a specialty of catching home runs. A little later, Tommy Henrich headed one "surely" into the right-field stands, a modest hit of 340 feet. Old Dixie Walker just stood there and plucked it off the home-run tree. It's a wonder he didn't put it in his mouth and taste it.

From the Bronx, from Queens, from Flushing and Jamaica and, yes, from Brooklyn this largest series crowd of history had come to see the Prince finish off his feast. But there was the Pauper at the victory board as series records now mean no more than the clipping of a fingernail.

We thought we had seen the ultimate last year with the Cardinals beating the Red Sox, but the department of worrying-about-your-ulcers has now taken command.

Allie Reynolds was knocked out and Joe Page was the losing Yank pitcher. Vic Lombardi and Ralph Branca were hit hard. And, in a parade of 10 hurlers, who should come in at the finish. You're right, of course—Hugh Casey. He came in when the passing of another minute would have seen the game called because the shadows were ominously long and, if you lit a cigaret, the glow of the match enveloped the fellow sitting next to you.

A flurry of two-base hits got the Dodgers out in front, 4-0, in the third. Then Yankee power took charge and little Vic Lombardi heard the call of the bench for the second time. Sherm Lollar doubled to left and reliever Karl Drews fanned after Lollar reached third on a passed ball.

Jorgensen kicked Stirnweiss' roller and Henrich, Lindell, DiMaggio, Johnson and Bobby Brown, batting for first sacker Jack Phillips, drilled clean singles off Lombardi and the relieving Branca. It was 4-4.

In the fourth, with Aaron Robinson on third and Henrich on first by virtue of singles, Yogi Berra clipped a single inside first that made it 5-4, and brought an eruption from the Dodgers, who claimed it was foul.

Eddie Stanky threw glove and hat on the ground as he stormed at Umpire Eddie Rommel and, in anything but the series, he would have been tossed out and heavily fined.

Joe Page was pitching now, old 55-game Joe with the easy delivery and good control. The Brooklyns have made their bid and fallen back; just a ball game now; Page'll hold 'em, said Yankee fans. Even the turbulent Dodger rooters were quiet.

So came the sixth and from that never-exhausted reservoir of Dodger hustle and fight sprang the rally which up-ended this strange contest.

Bruce Edwards singled to left and Carl Furillo

doubled to the same spot. In came Cookie Lavagetto to delirious cheers. This time the spoiler flied to right and Edwards scored the tying run. Bobby Bragan, a catcher, made his debut by doubling to left for Branca and Stanky singled to left center.

They took Page out then. From the bullpen in right center, strode the pod-fronted, once heroic form of Bobo Buck Newsom. Reese hit him for a single to left center and two more were over and it was 8-5. After this, Newsom, Vic Raschi and Charley Wensloff flattened the Flatbush Fusilliers.

Gionfriddo's miracle catch came in the sixth with Joe Hatten pitching and Walker's homer-stopper on Henrich led off the seventh. Nothing doing in the eighth. But the ninth? That's another matter.

Into the darkness, Bill Johnson rammed a single to left and Hatten walked George McQuinn. Here it was they hollered for Casey, and Casey came shuffling in from left center, taking his sweet time, for he is a man who loves the shadows. He got Phil Rizzuto on a fly to center field.

Aaron Robinson then punched a short single to left and the bases were filled as the crowd sensed the kill. Up to hit came Lonnie Frey, ironically enough, a former Brooklyn player. He hit a sharp hopper to Jackie Robinson and Jack threw to second, forcing Robinson as Johnson crossed the plate.

Working with the caution which accompanies the guardianship of an individual series cut of $7,000, Casey got Snuffy Stirnweiss to hit right back to the mound. And a seventh and deciding game in this classic of insanity was born.

A Yankee fan just passed in front of my typewriter. He grinned with one corner of his mouth and muttered—"Just tell 'em that God is on the Dodgers' side."

Could be.

1949

*As it turned out, the Dodger fortunes had
not yet shifted; despite the heroics of Cookie
Lavagetto and Al Gionfriddo, the Yankees still
won the 1947 World Series in seven games.*

*Two years later the same teams were at it
again. Burt Shotton had returned as the Brooklyn manager after a half-season hiatus the
previous year, while Casey Stengel was in his
first year at the helm for the Yankees.*

*The Yankees won the opener of the 1949
Series, 1-0, on a home run by Tommy Henrich
in the last of the ninth. The Dodgers hoped
to even the series with Preacher Roe on the
mound in Game Two:*

New York, October 6—The bustle-and-mustache cup
World Series of 1949 is all even today. The Brooklyn
Dodgers squared it up Thursday in the second game at
Yankee Stadium with a 1 to 0 victory over the New
York Yankees.

The Bombers had won the opening battle Wednesday by an identical score.

It was another pitching battle which must have
summoned the spirits of Christy Mathewson and
Three-Fingered Brown, stars of a day when tight
baseball was the tradition, to hover in admiration over
the victorious Elwin Roe and the almost-as-superb
Vic Raschi of the Yankees.

Brooklyn's skinny, sad-faced "Preacher" Roe stood
in his pitching pulpit and delivered a mound sermon
from the text, "Thou shalt not score."

And as he blanked the Yankees, more World Series
history was made, to wit:

This is the third time a series has started with two shutouts. (The others were in 1905 and 1921; both times, the score was 3 to 0.)

Thursday's was the third 1 to 0 series game in 16 years, the opener Wednesday having been the second.

There stood Roe, a curve-balling cadaver, looking like a fair-sized breeze would blow him over—but the Yankees couldn't do it.

They had chances, and it was in those chances that the day's drama lay. Brooklyn also looked opportunity in the face several times, and was stared at coldly by that fickle dame.

Where Wednesday's game was virtually thrill-less perfection, the hand of human frailty kept jogging the Thursday classic.

Twice errors put Roe into trouble, while the Yankee outfield kept threatening to place Raschi in a situation he couldn't throw himself out of.

In the end, though, the run the Dodgers scored in the second inning was all they needed, and 70,053 pew-holders went home clammily damp with frustrations or with joy, depending on their sympathies.

The setting was an expectant one for New York in the fifth, when Jerry Coleman doubled with one out, and again in the seventh, when Bill Johnson singled and stole, with two out, on a sleeping Pee Wee Reese. The Dodger shortstop had neglected to cover Roy Campanella's perfect throw on a delayed steal.

Roe outrode those tough moments and went into an eighth inning which turned out to be a test for the nerves of a pitching Frankenstein.

John Mize went in to bat for catcher Charley Silvera and led off with a single to right field. Snuffy Stirnweiss ran for him and Bobby Brown pinch-batted for Raschi.

But Roe fanned Brown with a lovely knee-high third strike.

Then Scooter Rizzuto bunted. He placed the ball so perfectly to the left of the mound that it eluded Roe's fingers as he grabbed frantically for it. He fumbled, and two men were on.

Now cheers rolled over the stadium and cascaded up the Bronx river valley. For Tommy Henrich was at bat—the homer hero of Wednesday, the old pro. Henrich fouled pitch after pitch, and finally got the count to 3-2. But Roe never gave him anything inside the middle, and finally he got Tommy out on a harmless fly to left field.

Up strode then the iron-muscled Hank Bauer to smash a blue dart toward third. Spider Jorgensen, who is built on the lines of Reddy Kilowatt, harnessed it and threw to second for the forceout.

The fans were limp then—nearly as limp as they had been in the second, when Brooklyn scored the run that won, and should have had more.

In that inning, Jackie Robinson rammed a racy liner to left for two bases and galloped to third after Gene Hermanski's foul had been caught by Coleman in right field. Marv Rackley, who later had to leave the game with a sore back, tapped weakly to third for the second out, and Jackie held third.

Then Gil Hodges made Flatbush come to life with a sizzling single between third and short, and Robinson loped in.

Even after that eighth inning, Roe wasn't out of trouble.

Joe DiMaggio led off the ninth by beating out an infield hit. But John Lindell struck out on a fast sinker. Bill Johnson popped to Robinson and Jerry Coleman flied easily to the substituting Mike McCormick in right field.

DiMaggio was marooned on first base, the game was over, the series was squared and Brooklyn fans swooned in ecstacy.

Friday? Well, it will be at Brooklyn now for three days.

1950

*The 1949 World Series ended in victory for
the Yankees once again. It wasn't until 1955
that the Dodgers would experience a world
championship of their own.*

*Meanwhile, the Yankees continued win-
ning. Their 1949 Series win was the beginning
of five consecutive world titles. In 1950, their
opponents were the "Whiz Kids," the Philadelphia Phillies, who had won their first National
League pennant in 35 years.*

*Halsey reports on the second and fourth
games of that series:*

Philadelphia, Pa. Oct. 5—Allie Reynolds and Joe
DiMaggio, two famous authors of popular thrillers,
wrote the Philadelphia Story here Thursday afternoon—a 2 to 1, 10-inning victory for the New York
Yankees over the Philadelphia Phillies.

The story was a tragedy for all loyal Philadelphians.
They now have lost the first two games of the World
Series to the defending champs.

DiMaggio's home run into deep left-center field in
the tenth inning sent the shining young Robin
Roberts to a heart-breaking defeat as 32,600 fans
mourned in brotherly misery.

The iron-hearted work of Reynolds, Yankee pitcher, completed the triumph. This morning the Bronx
Bombers, who have chosen to win with finesse and
defense rather than the continuous rumbling of their
hickory cannon, need only two more triumphs to hold
the world championship for another year.

The series shifts to Yankee Stadium in New York
today.

Yesterday's beautiful ball game was marked by one of the all-time freaks of World Series play. Had it not been for an errant pebble, nestling somewhere near the feet of Jerry Coleman, Yankee second sacker, Reynolds would have joined Vic Raschi in a 1-0 victory and Roberts would have joined his teammate hurler, Jim Konstanty, on the agony road an inning sooner.

The Yankees had a 1-0 lead in the fifth inning. They had acquired it in the second when Coleman walked, Reynolds singled to right putting Jerry on third, and Gene Woodling singled to deep short.

Mike Goliat led off for the Phils in the fifth with a single, but Roberts, trying to sacrifice, popped out. Eddie Waitkus then hit the easiest kind of a slow bounder right to Coleman.

As Jerry got set for the catch and throw, that ball took a hop like an intoxicated kangaroo.

It bounced high beyond reach into right field, and Goliat scampered to third base.

Here was the break that could crack the nerves of a man of iron and arouse the sleeping power in the Philly attack.

The stands knew it and they shredded the air with mad screaming. It was up to Richie Ashburn, and Richie scored Goliat with a fly ball to Woodling in left field.

With the weight of such misfortune on his shoulders, Reynolds did well to escape with no more damage.

But wait! The Phillies had yet to compound the freakishness of this screwy inning. No sooner had their half of the inning ended and their red and white clad warriors taken the field than out came—the entire ground-keeping crew of a dozen men.

They hauled drags around the infield, they stomped

with heavy bars upon every lumpy spot, they pushed rollers, they swept.

It was as if the voice of conscience had said, "Here now, Phils, that's no way to score," or—more probably—the voice of prudence saying, "Here now, let's fix things up before the Yankees get a bounce like that."

The manicuring over, the umpires finally got the toilers off the diamond and Robin Roberts went into a stretch of brilliant pitching, more than matching the redoubtable Reynolds.

Here was a kid of 22, looking ever younger than he is, who had pitched four games in eight days through the hot finish of the National campaign.

He had worked extra innings in Brooklyn last Sunday to clinch the flag and now one extra inning again. Where Konstanty got in and out of trouble Wednesday, Reynolds did it yesterday.

In the eighth a double play pulled him free, and in the ninth Granny Hamner, who earlier had hit a triple, doubled to right center with only one out. Dick Whitman went in to bat for catcher Ken Silvestri and was purposely passed. The Yankee strategy was crowned with success, for Goliat hit a brisk grounder to the all-encompassing Phil Rizzuto at short and was doubled at first.

Roberts had retired the champs one-two-three in the ninth and had blanked DiMaggio, as had Konstanty Wednesday.

But this time the spark plug of the Yankees hit what he said was an inside "slider" and the ball dropped into the upper deck of the left-center bleachers about 385 feet from home.

That may be considerably farther from "home" than the Yanks are now. A victory today would erect a monumental barrier to Philly hopes.

*   *   *

New York, Oct. 7—The Yankees of New York still are the world champions of baseball.

They shouldered aside the Whiz Kids of Philadelphia, 5-2, here Saturday to win their 13th diamond diadem in 17 tries. It was the sixth time the Yankees have won the World Series in four-straight games.

Again calling on most of the weapons in the arsenal of baseball, the Yankees won behind the blond southpaw, Ed (Whitey) Ford.

As excitable as Ole Bull, standing in Minneapolis' Loring Park, Whitey was rescued by Allie Reynolds in the ninth. Gene Woodling dropped a fly ball from the bat of Andy Seminick to let in two runs and Mike Goliat singled before Reynolds came in.

Reynolds, the chunky Cherokee from Oklahoma, promptly fanned pinch-hitter Stan Lopata to set off a delirious Yankee celebration, a procedure that is becoming depressingly monotonous to National league foemen.

Gambling his autumn baseball life, Eddie Sawyer, the philosophical Phil boss, started young Bob Miller, thin as a flounder. His mates promptly got him into trouble and "konstant" Jim Konstanty came in during the first frame.

Goliat fumbled Woodling's grounder near second base and Phil Rizzuto grounded out. Bomber guns boomed then. Yogi Berra laced a single to right, scoring Woodling. Berra went all the way to third as the sore-ankled Seminick hobbled after a wild pitch.

Joe DiMaggio unraveled a screamer into right field for two bases, tallying the Yogi. In came Konstanty with that weaving stride of his, and young Miller walked with head down into the autumn shadows.

Konstanty was his normal self, as steady as time. Ford knew few moments of anxiety. When they came up, it was the Philadelphia Story—with additional chapters.

In the fourth, the singling Del Ennis and Granny Hamner were on first and third. Seminick hit to Mize near first base. Big Jawn touched the bag retiring Seminick and fired home. Berra did not forget to touch Ennis as he tried to score. It was a double play, almost a replica of the incident between Detroit and Cleveland where catcher Aaron Robinson was the victim.

In the sixth Ennis lived on the first Yankee error of the series, a fumble by Bobby Brown at third base. But Dick Sisler hit sharply to Jerry Coleman at second for a double play.

Konstanty, sharp as an owl to this point, suddenly became common clay. Berra jarred him for a mighty home run into the right-field seats. DiMaggio was hit by a pitch and Brown reached the open spaces of right-center field with a three-base hit.

Brown came home when Sisler went back to the 380-foot mark to snare Hank Bauer's sky ball.

So it was 5-0 for the merciless men of Manhattan. Their bench was a duplication of a kids' Sunday school picnic. They were oblivious to the fact 68,098 fans were watching them and that possibly half that number wanted the National Leaguers to win.

A pinch hitter relieved Konstanty in the eighth and, taking the mound for the Phils, was Robin Roberts, losing hero of Thursday's 10-inning game at Philadelphia.

Roberts got the Yanks out in the eighth and Ford stepped to the rim of glory. One inning to go and a shutout in a World Series game in his first half year in the majors.

Puddin'-head Jones hit a single and then Ford hit
Ennis on the leg. Stengel strode back and forth in the
dugout. Ford caused Sisler to force Ennis and struck
out the dangerous Granny Hamner. Then Seminick
belted one with all the power in his bow-legged frame.

It looked like a home run but there was Woodling
staggering backward to the running track, 10 feet in
front of the left-field boxes.

Woodling wavered, reached, got the ball partly in
his glove and dropped it. Over the plate roared two
runs and hopes of a shutout.

So Casey called in Allie Reynolds. And Lopata was
right up Reynolds' alley.

1957

Halsey's last entry into a "Best Sports Stories" publication, this appeared in the <u>Women's Section</u> of the <u>Minneapolis Sunday Tribune</u> September 15, 1957 and was entitled 'How to Enjoy Football':

There was once a Minnesota football player whose mother never had seen him play. She was rather reluctant to see him, too, because she had heard football was a brutal game and she would just as soon her boy, Robert, would concentrate on physical therapy or on a course like they have at Stanford, called something like "movie appreciation."

But he finally prevailed on her to see a game. Now in those days one man lay on his stomach to hold the ball for the man kicking off. Robert had this little chore, so down he lay. The kicker measured his steps, ran forward and gave the ball a mighty, end-over-end boot down the field.

Up in the stands his mother sobbed, "Oh, my Lord, there goes Robert's head." She fainted dead away.

Now I do not believe any of you ladies would thus succumb nowadays. For one thing, you'll notice nobody holds the ball on the kickoff; it's booted off a tee.

A male friend, who claims he has suffered much from taking the Little Lady to gridiron conflicts, insists women think of related items, rather than what is unfolding before them. For instance, there was the gal who, upon getting her first glimpse of Memorial Stadium when emerging from the ramp, exclaimed, "Oh look at the pretty grass."

You must become hardened to things. They call the football a pigskin and kick it around. Many piggy wraiths probably are writhing in horror at the way their once precious hide sometimes is fumbled.

Among first things, it is very nice if you will learn the songs of the school whose games you attend. At Minnesota there is the "Rouser," "Minnesota Hail to Thee," and the "Fight Song," John Philip Sousa's masterpiece, etc.

If you have even some vague idea, you will eliminate the repetition of one faux pas that was committed at the stadium recently. First the band played "Hail to Thee." Then came the "Rouser." Our friend asked her man, "What are they playing now?" He told her. "Oh dear," she blushed, "I just got through singing that."

Many experts say the most enjoyment can be derived by taking your eyes off the man carrying the ball—at least once in a while. Now this is advice also given to such superior beings as other men and even visiting coaches and players. Like all good advice, it is seldom followed, so I see no point in you gals bothering about it.

If you do, however, watch the blockers. They are the men who run ahead of the ball carrier to clear his way. The fact that the ball carrier often will trip over them and fall down, thus making it unnecessary for the opposition to tackle him, is just part of the game. (To coaches it is known as a contributory factor in the raising of ulcers.)

Presumably, you are filled with the old school spirit, even though your only venture on learning's seas was grade school 3,000 miles away. Now the lady or gentleman next to you may also be filled with spirit. Sometimes they conceal it in a shoulder flask and great used to be the art of inserting a straw into said flask and, under the guise of examining a rip in the arm pit, such a warm 86-proof bit of sustenance.

This, of course, is frowned upon by college authorities and stadium ushers.

It will aid greatly in preserving surrounding tempers if you will do your standing and utterances of, "Oh, there's Persephone down there. Still wearing last year's coat," etc., between halves.

The referee is one of four or five men wearing zebra-like shirts and white pants. They carry red handkerchiefs used for blowing the nose and for throwing. You will hear the loudspeaker blare, "There's a flag on the play!" This means somebody has committed an infraction and an official signals it by throwing the red hankie on the ground. You may think it an unsanitary procedure.

If he penalizes your team five or 15 yards, you may show you're well informed by remarking to your escort, "the blankety-blank so-and-so must be getting paid by the other side."

If, however, he gives the other guys a penalty and it's first down for your team, your male pal will think you're real hep to the game if you state: "There's an official who's certainly on the ball, isn't he?"

There are three kinds of kicking besides your friend's expressed opinion of the seats they've sold him. There is the punt, the placekick, and the dropkick.

The punt is where the man holds the ball, drops it, kicks it before it hits the ground. Watch the ends of the kicker's team: they are supposed to be first down the field, ready to tackle the man who catches the ball. Watch the guards and tackles who, after the kick, are supposed to do the same. So is the center after he gets up.

Watch the linemen on the other team. Some will rush through, trying to block the punt. Some who don't go through will form interference for their guy who catches the ball. Watch the officials, watch the punter, watch the men in front of the punter, watch the officials, see how they fan out to cover the action.

Watch all this—at once, mind you—and you'll understand why coaches and scouts are not considered top insurance risks and often have their own private wards in mental homes. They're trying to watch it all at once, too.

The placekick is where they try to kick the ball over the goal post crossbar after a touchdown or for a field goal. The dropkick is made by dropping the ball and booting it the instant it touches the ground. The dropkick is now seen as often as high-buttoned shoes.

When a player throws a long forward pass and it is fumbled or hits the ground, do not cheer. It is not a three-base hit or a home run. If your side does it and you cheer, you are not likely to be included in the cocktail party.

You may get excited as all get out when one of your boys runs for dear life, nobody laying a hand on him as he heads straight for the sidelines. Don't be an idiot and yell at this; his run is as valuable as the one in your stocking.

When there is a rest period and a fellow in white runs out with a bottle to a group of players, don't plead: "Please send for that man to come up to our section. I'm thirsty." "That man" is the trainer or one of his assistants and not a stadium vendor.

Football is a rough game. The players expect their lumps. They take it all with admirable spunk and you'd be surprised at the humorous touches that can creep out, too.

There was the time a Gopher was knocked cold in a pile-up. As he resumed breathing, a trainer asked him "How are you?" And he replied, "Oh, I'm all right, but how did all those people get back up in the stands?"

Bibliography

Barton, George A. *My Lifetime in Sports.* Minneapolis: The Olympic Press, 1957.

Briere, Tom. "Former sports colleagues eulogize Hall." *Minneapolis Tribune*, January 1, 1978, p. 1C.

Caray, Harry with Bob Verdi. *Holy Cow!* New York: Villard Books, 1989.

Cohen, Dan. *Undefeated: The Life of Hubert Humphrey.* Minneapolis: Lerner Publications Company, 1978.

Cullum, Dick. "Gophers Escape Fire: Many Treated For Smoke in Hotel Blaze." *Minneapolis Journal*, September 24, 1936, p. 1.

DeHaven, Bob. *55 Years Before the Mike.* Minneapolis: James D. Thueson, 1985.

Egan, John. "Twins anniversary incomplete without Hall." *Argus Leader*, July 22, 1986, p. 1C.

El-Hai, Jack. "Adventures In Wonderland." *Mpls.-St. Paul*, August 1988, pp. 112-115.

Gordon, Dick. "Leaving behind a legend as long as the 'longest' home run." *Minneapolis Star*, May 13, 1978, p. 4.

Grawert, Don. "Holy Cow! The Legend of Halsey Hall." *Wold News,* Fall 1984, pp. 10-11.

Haeg, Larry, Jr. *Sixty Years Strong: The Story of One of America's Great Radio Stations, 1924-84.* Minneapolis: WCCO Radio, 1984.

Hage, George S. *Newspapers of the Frontier 1849-1860.* St. Paul: Minnesota Historical Society, 1967.

Hardman, Benedict E. *Everybody Called Him Cedric.* Minneapolis: Twin City Federal Savings & Loan Association, 1970.

Holbert, Allan. "As Baseball Goes, So Goes Halsey." *Minneapolis Sunday Tribune*, July 10, 1966, p. 1.

Johnson, Charles. *History of the Metropolitan Stadium and Sports Center*. Minneapolis: Midwest Federal, 1971.

Johnson, Ron D. "Halsey Puffs Past Fifty-Yard Line." *Minnesota Motorist*, January 1969, p. 10.

Kirshenbaum, Jerry. "And Here, to Bring You the Play by Play..." *Sports Illustrated*, September 13, 1971, pp. 33-43.

Lee, Betty. "Wonderland Didn't Last Long." *The Longfellow Messenger*, September 1984, p. 1.

Letofsky, Irv. "Halsey Hall: As popular as the first day of spring." *Minneapolis Tribune*, July 7, 1976, p. 1C.

Marling, Karal Ann. "Thrills and Nostalgia: The Amusement Parks of Hennepin County." *Hennepin History*, Fall 1990, pp. 13-22.

Marsh, Irving T. and Edward Ehre, eds. *Best Sports Stories*. New York: E. P. Dutton & Company, Inc., 1947, 1948, 1950, 1951, 1958.

Meusey, Jim. "The Happy World of Halsey Hall." *St. Louis Park Sun*, December 9, 1971, pp. 1-2.

Moore, Dave. *A Member of the Family*. Minneapolis-St. Paul: The Lazear Press, 1986.

Morison, Bradley L. *Sunlight On Your Doorstep: The Minneapolis Tribune's First Hundred Years*. Minneapolis: Ross & Haines, Inc., 1966.

Murphy, Terry. "Halsey Hall, 79, dies at his home." *Minneapolis Tribune*, January 1, 1978, p. 1A.

Nichols, Max. "Minnesotans Pack Hall, Raise Cheers In Salute to Halsey." *The Sporting News*, July 30, 1966, p. 12.

O'Grady, Donald J. *History at Your Door 1849-1983: The Pioneer Press and Dispatch*. St. Paul: Northwest Publications, Inc., 1983.

Pāpas, Al, Jr. *Gopher Sketchbook*. Minneapolis: Nodin Press, 1990.

Parker, John, ed. *Who Was Who in the Theatre: 1912-1976*. Detroit: Gale Research Company, 1978.

Rainbolt, Richard. *Gold Glory*. Wayzata, MN: Ralph Turtinen Publishing Company, 1972.

Reusse, Patrick. "At 76, Hall in 'pretty good shape'." *St. Paul Sunday Pioneer Press,* December 15, 1974, p. 9.

Sarjeant, Charles F., ed. *The First Forty: The Story of WCCO Radio*. Minneapolis: WCCO Radio, 1964.

Shama, Dave. "Holy Cow! Where's Halsey?" *Greater Minneapolis*, August 1975, pp. 32-36.

Soucheray, Joe. "Nothing could dampen Halsey Hall's dry wit." *Minneapolis Tribune*, November 15, 1981, p. 2C.

Staples, Loring M. *The West Hotel Story 1884-1940: Memories of Past Splendor*. Minneapolis: Carlson Printing Company, 1979.

Stewart, A. J. D., ed. *The History of the Bench and Bar of Missouri*. St. Louis: Legal Publishing Company, 1898.

Storrs, Caryl B. "Vistin' Round in Minnesota." *Minneapolis Tribune*, July 1, 1916, p. 18.

Trennery, Walter N. *Murder in Minnesota: A Collection of True Cases*. St. Paul: Minnesota Historical Society Press, 1985.

Turtinen, Ralph, ed. *100 Years of Golden Gopher Football*. Minneapolis: Men's Intercollegiate Athletic Department of the University of Minnesota, 1981.

Williams, Bob and Chuck Hartley, ed. *Good Neighbor to the Northwest 1924-1974*. Minneapolis: WCCO Radio, 1974.

Young, William C. *Famous Actors and Actresses on the American Stage*. New York: R. R. Bowker Company, 1975.

Index

Elliott, Babe, 33
Emmaus, Pennsylvania, 113
Empire Theatre, Boston, 12
Engdahl, Frank, 97
English, Elwood (Woody), 202, 203
Ennis, Del, 222, 223
Enroth, Dick, 67, 70
Erickson, Roger, 64-65
Evenson, E. W., 47
Evening Journal, The, 16
Excelsior Amusement Park, 25, 125

Fairmount School, Duluth, 114
Fairview Hospital, Minneapolis, 121
Fargo High School, 113
Fargo, North Dakota, 113
Farrell, Henry L., 35
Federal Communications Commission, 65
Fenner, Bob, 38
Fergus Falls, Minnesota, 15-16
Fergus Falls Telegram, 15-16
Fesler, Wes, 69
Fields, W. C., 77, 158
Fitzgerald, Eddie, 33, 140
Flood, Curt, 173
Florence Hotel, Missoula, 155
Florida State League, 94
Flower, Caully, 35
Ford, Ed (Whitey), 76, 221, 222, 223
Fort Snelling National Cemetery, 187

Fort Walton Beach, Florida, 94
Fowler, Bob, 183
Fox, Howard, 159-160, 163-164
Fox, Nellie, 104
Foxx, Jimmy, 202, 203
Freeman, Orville, 85
Frey, Linus (Lonnie), 213
Furillo, Carl, 206, 210, 211, 212

Gaff, Glen, 31
Gaffke, Fabian, 100
Galan, August (Augie), 206, 207
Gammons, Earl, 61
Garfield, James A., 14
Garske, Jack, 56
Gehrig, Lou, 42, 43, 53
General Hospital, 186, 187
General Mills, 67
Gentile, Jim, 57
Getchell, Johnny, 108
Gibbons, Phantom Mike, 60
Gibbons, Tommy, 59-61, 67
Giel, Paul, 72-73, 86, 163, 177
Gierek, Edward, 189
Gill, Johnny, 145
Gionfriddo, Al, 210-211, 213, 214
Giuliani, Angelo, 54, 58, 108
Gmitro, Rudy, 68
Goheen, Francis X. (Moose), 33, 116, 177
Goliat, Mike, 219, 220, 221
Gomez, Vernon (Lefty), 93-94
Gonzalez, Mike, 203, 204
Gordon, Dick, 30-31, 49, 87, 161
Gostick, Glenn, 162
Grady, Mike, 92-93

Turner, Vi, 195
Twin Cities Free Press, 58, 105
Twin City Federal Saving &
  Loan, 169

Unique Theater, Minneapolis, 25
Union Association, 36
United States Amateur Hockey
  League, 32, 115
Uram, Andy, 68

Van Atta, Russ, 38
Veeck, Bill, 177, 178
Viken, Howard, 154
Village Nursing Home, New
  York, 27
Virginia High School, 29-30
Vocational High School, Minne-
  apolis, 26

Wagner, Honus, 53, 65
Waitkus, Eddie, 219
Walberg, George (Rube), 200, 201
Walker, Fred (Dixie), 207, 208,
  211, 213
Walsh, Ed, 40
Walt Disney World, 181
Wambsganss, Bill, 209
Wann, Paul, 70
War of 1812, 13
Warmath, Murray, 69, 73, 157
Warsaw, Poland, 189
Washington, D. C., 14, 15, 159
Washington Huskies, 71-72, 155
Washington Senators (1901-60),
  74, 75

Washington Senators (1961-71),
  77
Watertown, South Dakota, 95
WCCO Radio, 61-81 *passim,* 92,
  130, 156, 170, 185, 192
WCCO Television, 56, 62, 169
Wensloff, Charley, 213
Werness Brothers Funeral
  Chapel, 193
West High School, Minneapolis,
  110
West Hotel, 17
White, Euphemia deLuce
  (maternal grandmother), 11, 18
White, Henry P. (maternal
  grandfather), 11
White House, 126
Whitman, Dick, 207, 220
Widseth, Ed, 68
Wilkinson, Charles (Bud), 68
Will, Lester, 35
Willard, Jess, 59
Williams, Rollie, 96
Williams, Ted, 51, 97, 145
Wilson, George, 145
Wilson, Lewis (Hack), 40, 202
Wingfield, Fred, 38
Winona, Minnesota, 87
Winter, Max, 177, 178-179
Wisconsin Badgers, 92, 96
Wisconsin State Journal, 73
Wisconsin—Stout, University of,
  108
WLOL Radio, 55, 70
Wolff, Bob, 75, 76, 77, 89, 160
Wonderland Amusement Park,
  25, 125

Woodling, Gene, 219, 221
World War I, 26, 29, 33
Worthington, Al, 176
Worthington High School, 29
Wrigley Field, 42, 199
WTCN Radio, 156
WTCN Television, 75, 81, 192
WTMB Radio, 175

Yale University, 96
Yankee Stadium, 76, 89, 210,
    214, 218

Zeibert, Duke, 164-165
Ziebarth, E. W., 64, 170
Zimmerman, Jerry, 78-79